RHYTHM FROM WITHIN

CREATING MOVEMENT FROM AN INNER VOICE

michael philip manheim

PHOTOGRAPHY

SEE-SAW

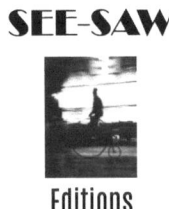

Editions

Also by Michael Philip Manheim

In A Labyrinth

Last House Standing, A Chapter*

See-Saw, A Sampler*

The Smoking Fifties*

Where My Spirit Guides Us*

*These books can be found on Amazon by scrolling to "books" in the search field and then entering "michael philip manheim."

For further information or permissions, including the leasing of reproduction rights, contact Michael Philip Manheim at http://www.michaelphilipmanheim.com/MPM-contact_form.php

Printed in the United States of America.

ISBN 978-0-9844803-7-1

Cover photograph: *Whispering Hope* ©2003
Back cover photograph: *Dancing Dryads* ©2002

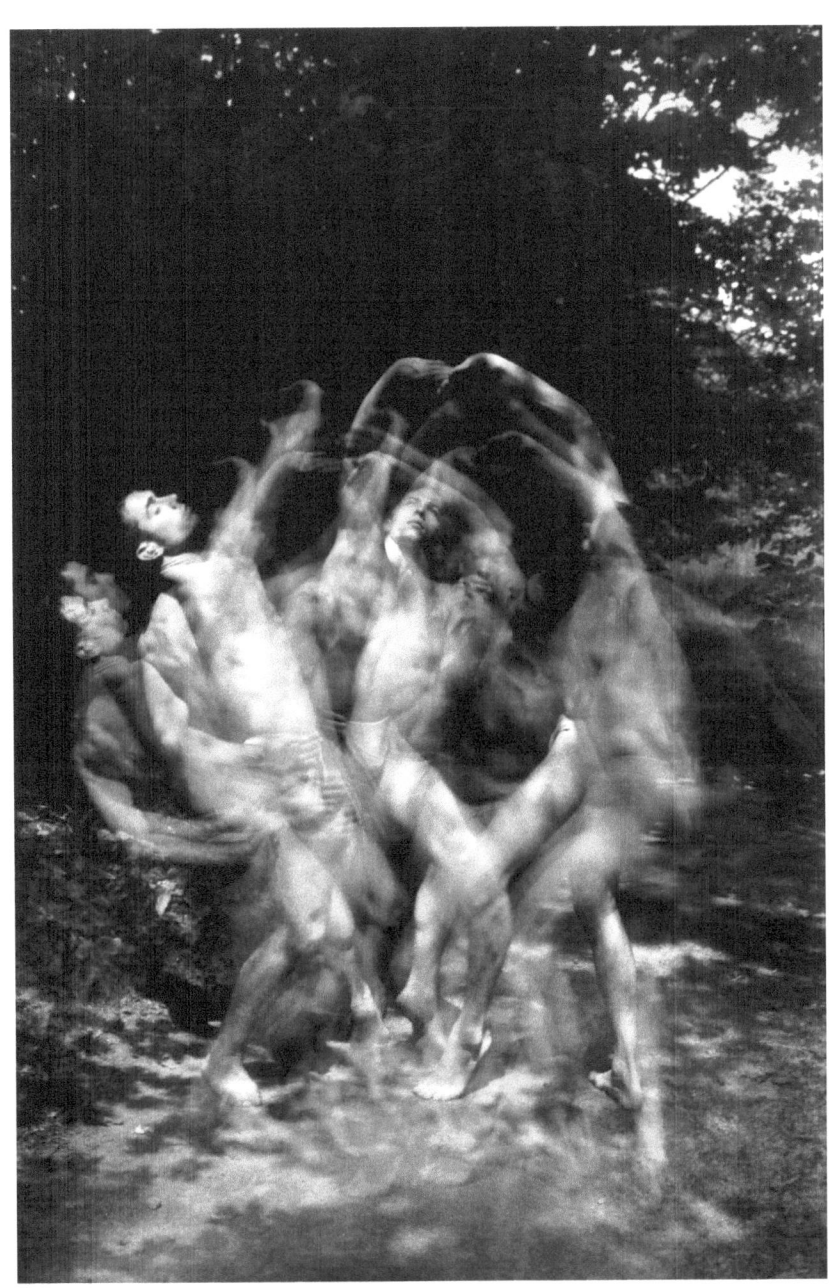

Men Dancers Saratoga Springs, New York 1999

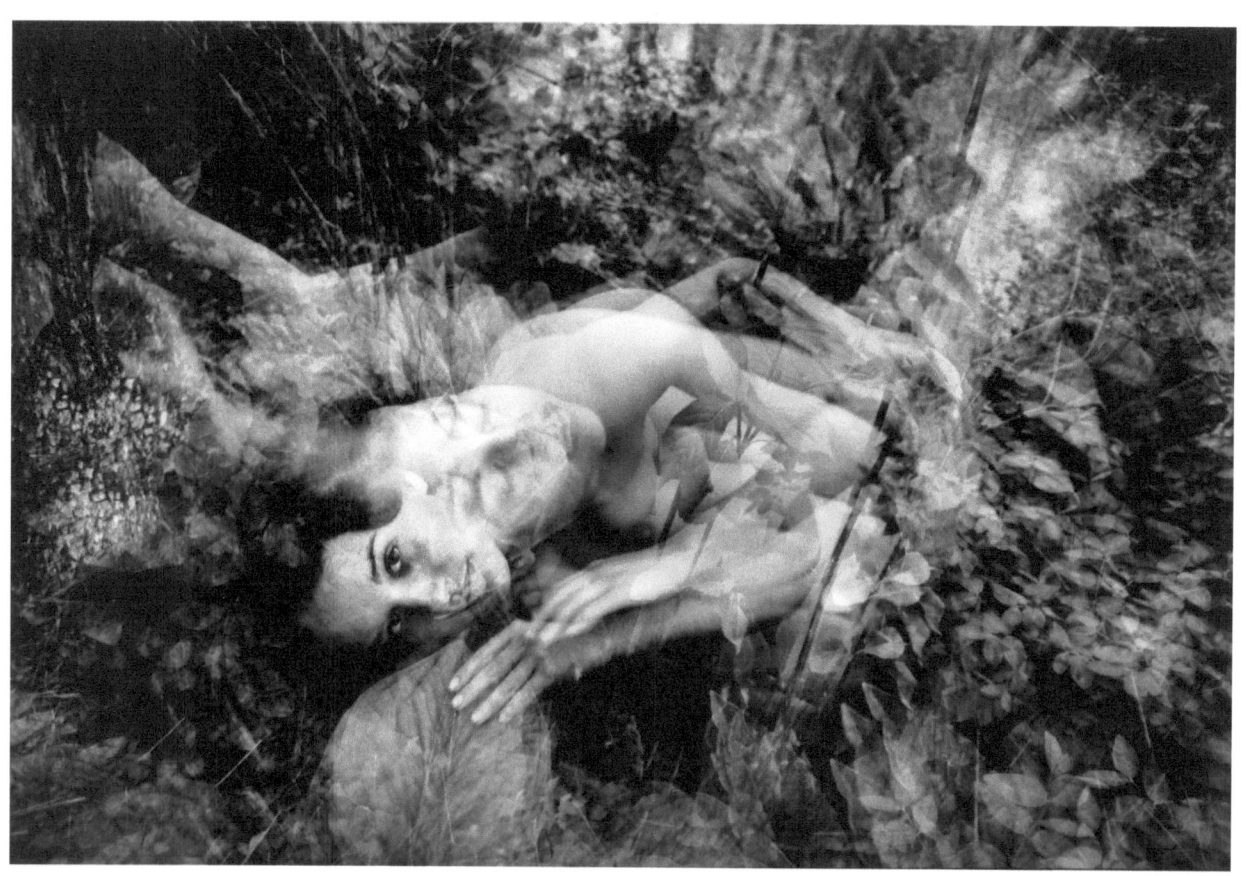

In My Dreams Lewiston, Maine 2002

Dedication

This book is dedicated to the driving force and nurturer of the Bates Dance Festival for 30 years. Laura Faure hosted me for four summer seasons at Bates College in Lewiston, Maine. She supported my photography much in the same manner that she encouraged the dance professionals who performed and taught, as well as the students who soaked up their lessons. Laura provided an encouraging atmosphere for us all, for each to find our own vision. I was delighted to invite participants for *Rhythm From Within* from both faculty and students, and some of our collaborations appear in this book.

Laura has now retired, turning over to her successor, Shoshona Currier, one of the nation's leading dance festivals. Shoni is adding her own deft touches in both maintaining and expanding the program.

I want to thank Laura, as well as all the dancers and dance companies represented in these pages, who have collaborated so wonderfully over the years with my project, including:

Bridgman/Packer

Delirious Dance

Kaori Ito

Leimay at Cave

Limon Dance Company

Maureen Fleming

Parsons Dance

Prometheus Dance Company

Robert Moses' Kin

Artist's Statement

This series developed out of my wanting to expand the possibilities of still photography through a new approach to the nude in nature. I had long felt that a beautiful body is a work of art by itself, so I didn't need to document that. Instead, I created and perfected my own method of in-camera multiple exposures and I sought out subjects not for their outward appearance, but for their ability to turn feelings into movement.

I scouted locations in nature where participants would feel safe to delve into their vulnerability, and to physically express their emotions. I asked my subjects to choose a spot, meditate on their surroundings, and spontaneously move as if they were alone. I didn't direct beyond initial encouragement, and I assured them that they could do nothing wrong. I trusted their intuition to bring out the human condition and make a connection with the Earth. We experimented, trying minimal costuming, then partial nudity, then full nudity. I reacted instinctively and reflexively. As they went into motion, I made many exposures onto each frame of film.

These overlaid images frequently created a sort of costume for my subjects. Rather than a literal representation of nudes in nature, these photographs conveyed the sensation of a body in motion, with a roundness, a dynamic, and a dimension that moved beyond a moment in time. A few individuals even metamorphosed into unrecognizable beings. No matter how different my subjects were from each other, they all displayed a plethora of emotions, and communicated them through the universal language of the body.

Intricate meshing with nature, complex depths of expression, intriguing effects and juxtapositions...all spontaneously appearing in the camera... after every session, editing was both difficult and a pleasure.

One reviewer called my method "risky photography," because there was no way to predict the outcome. The final images formed inside the camera—as multiple exposures layered on single frames—and I utilized only basic dodging and burning in the darkroom. There was no premeditation, just meditation that powered my exploration of the *Rhythm From Within*.

—Michael Philip Manheim

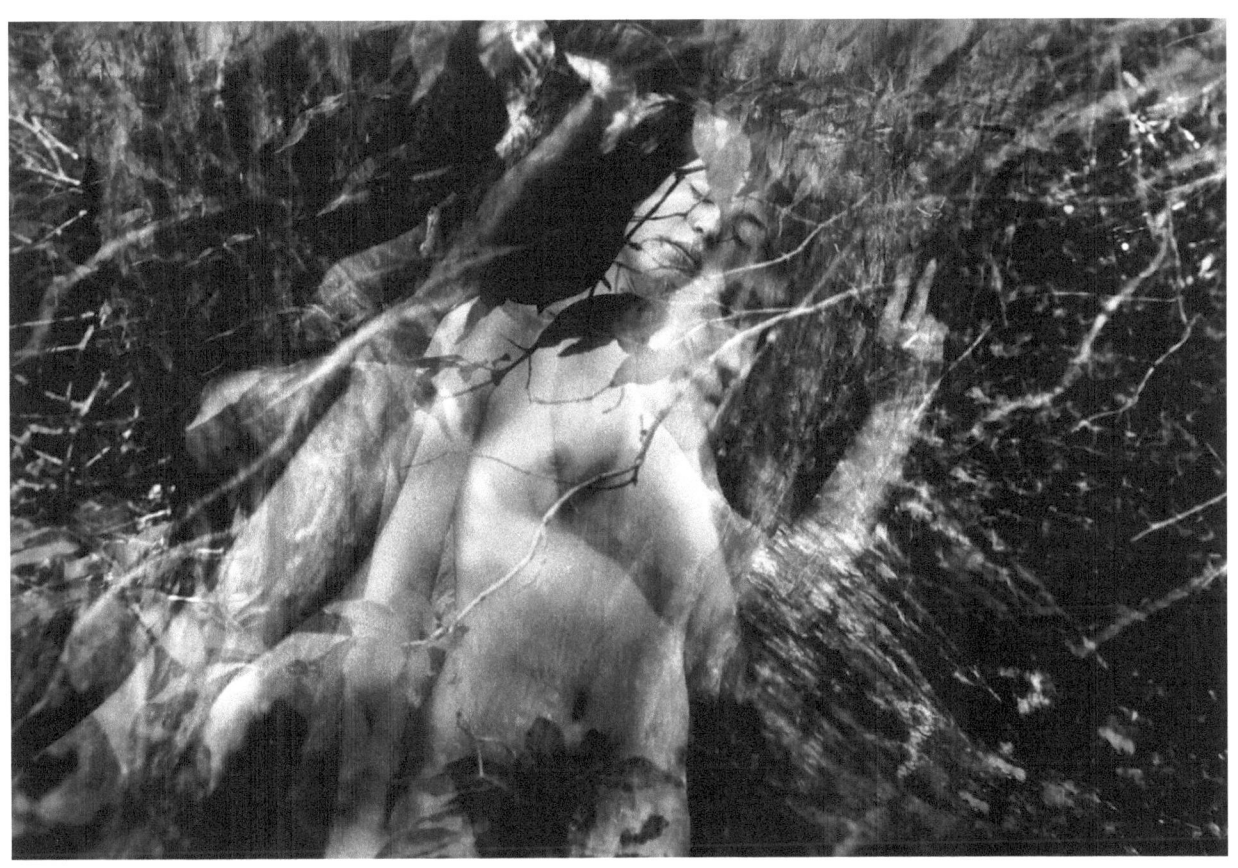

Elfin Conjuring South Hadley, Massachusetts 2004

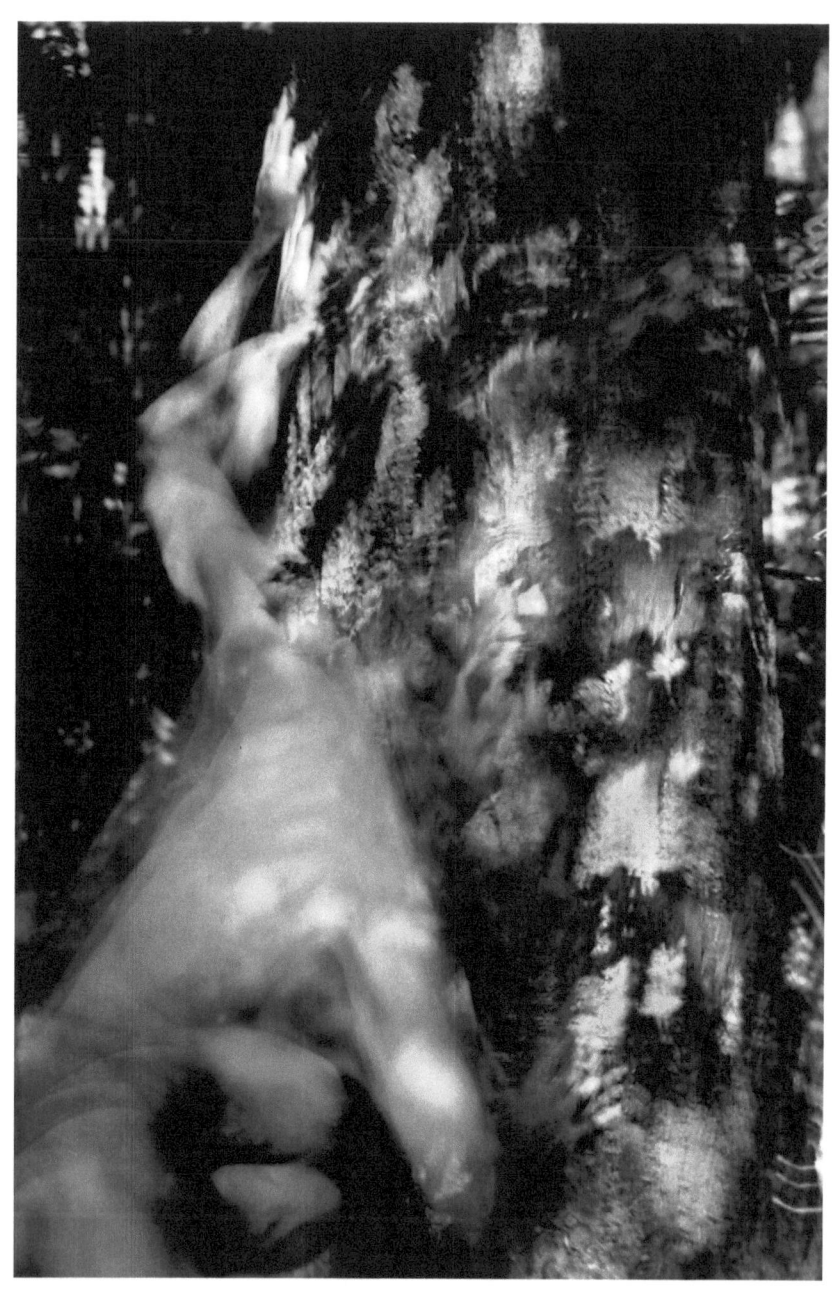

Apollo Appears Lewiston, Maine 2001

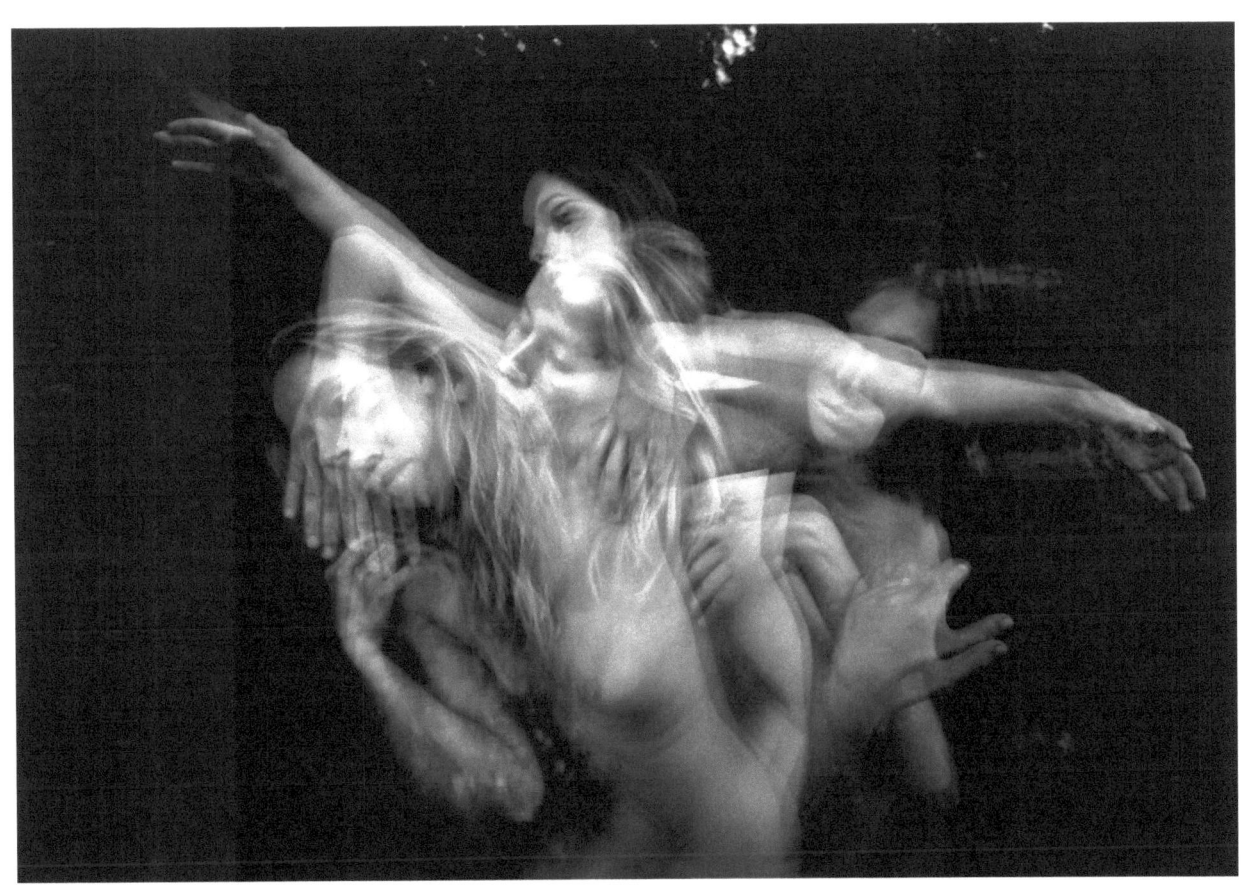

Full of Flight Lewiston, Maine 2002

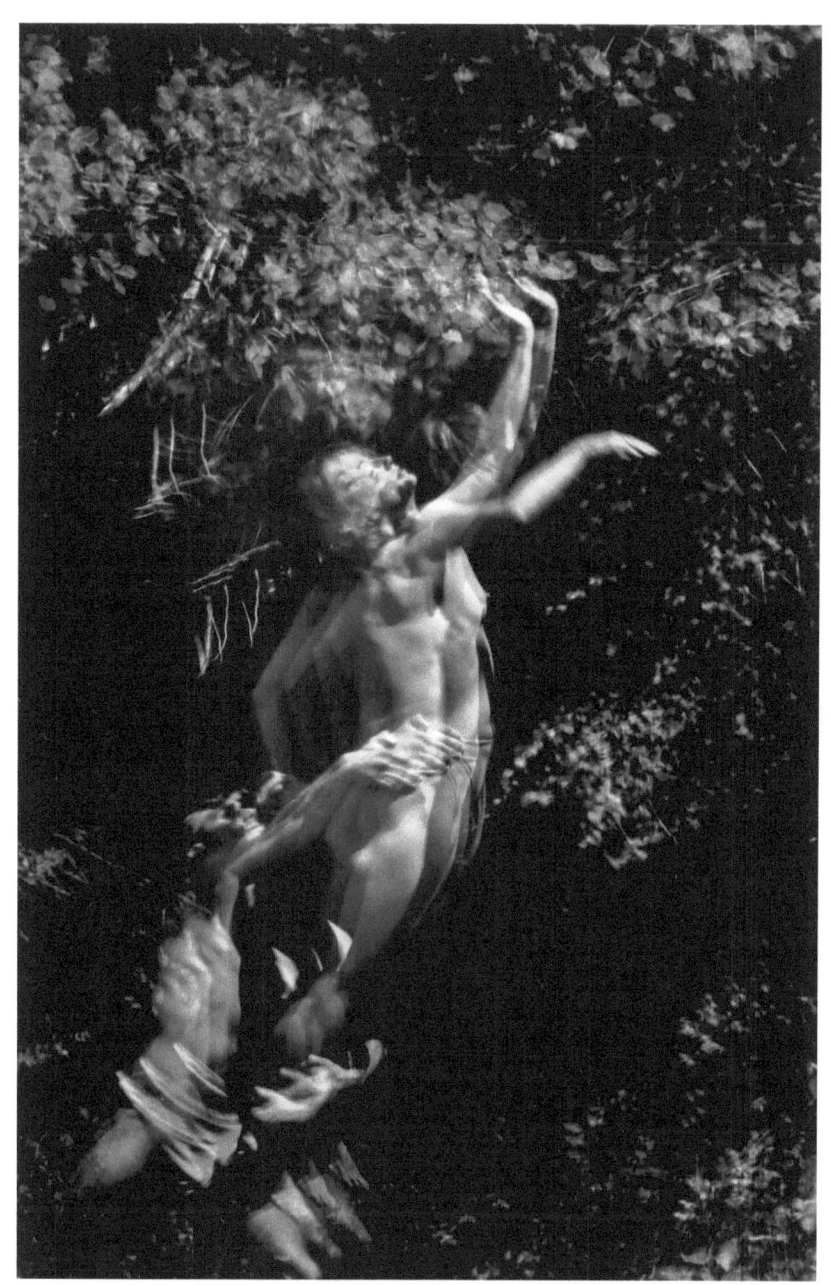

Forbidden Fruit Saratoga Springs, New York 1999

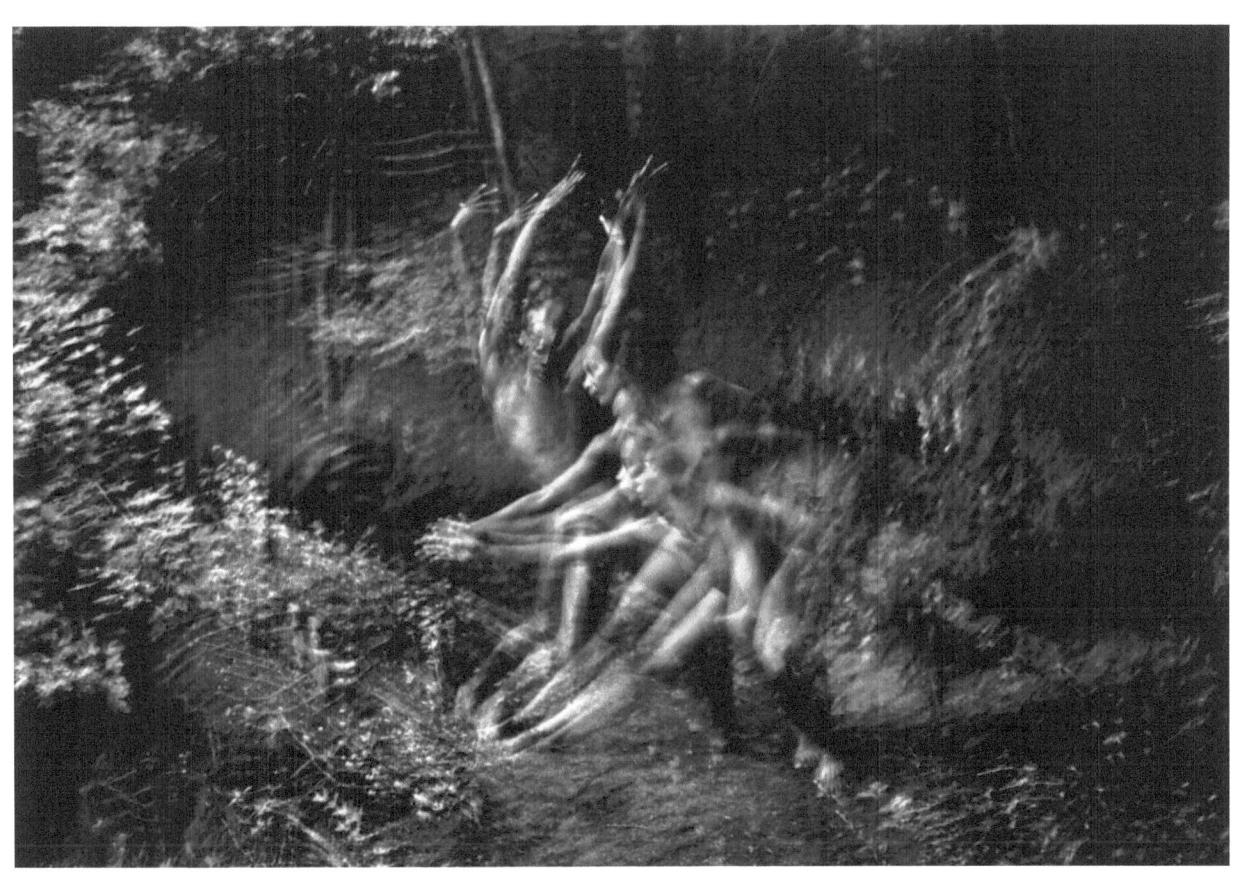

Riverbend Concord, Massachusetts 2000

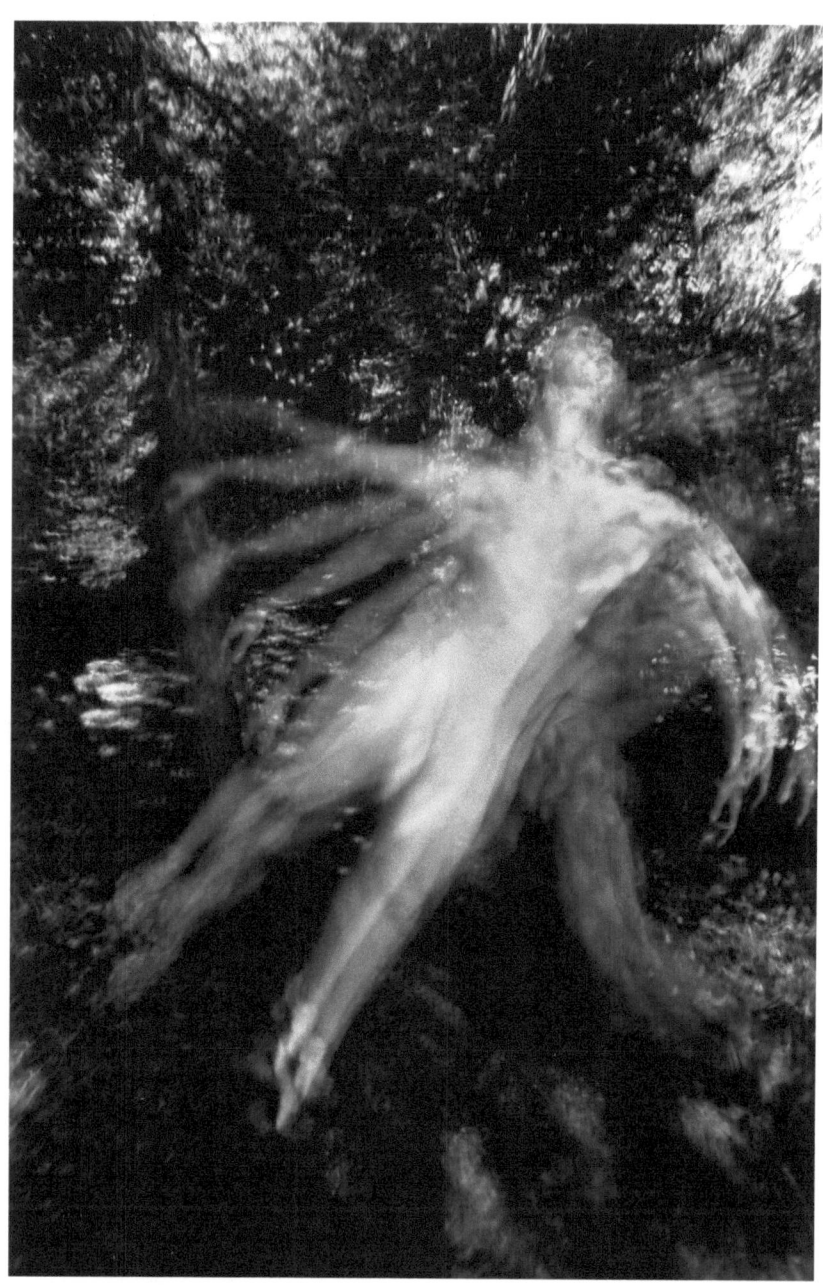

Icarus Becket, Massachusetts 1998

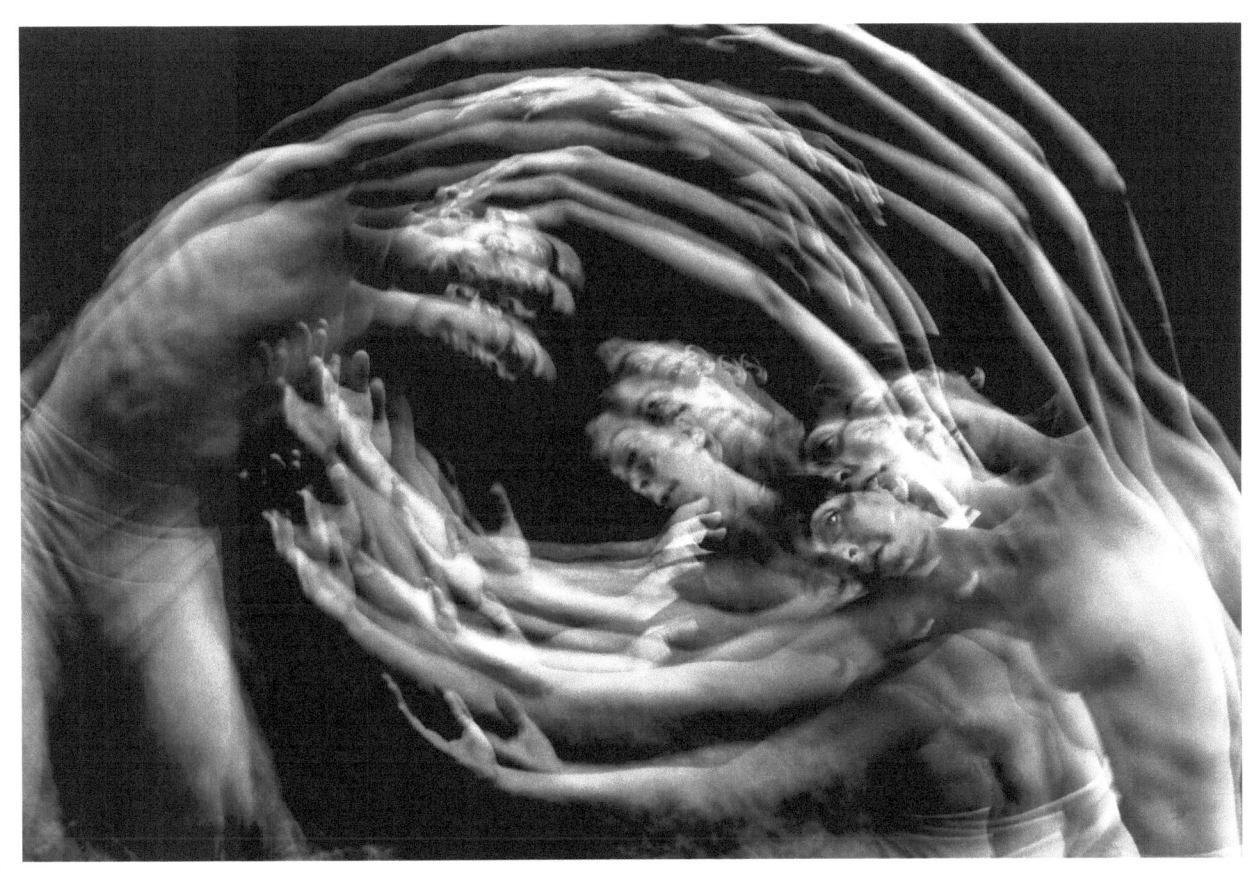

Cosmos Saratoga Springs, New York 1999

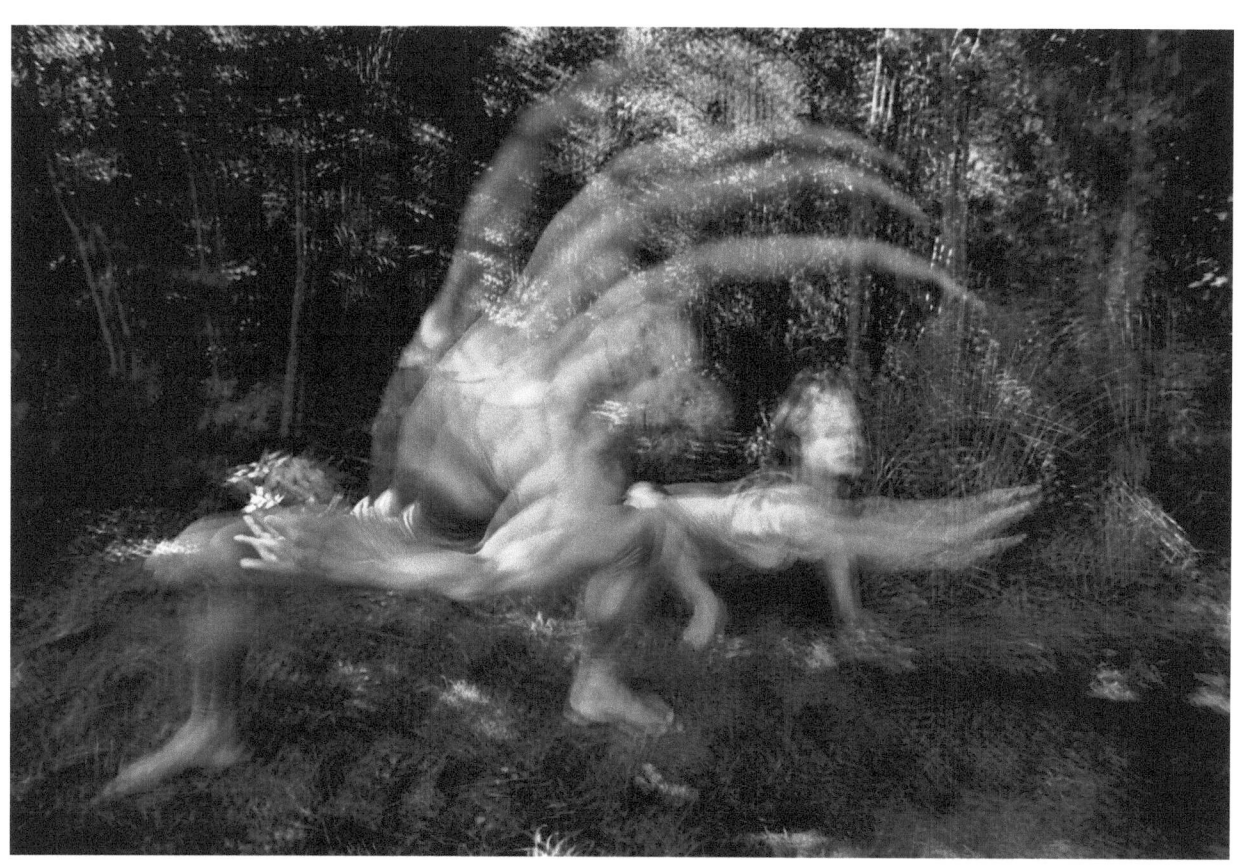

Bird Reach Becket, Massachusetts 1998

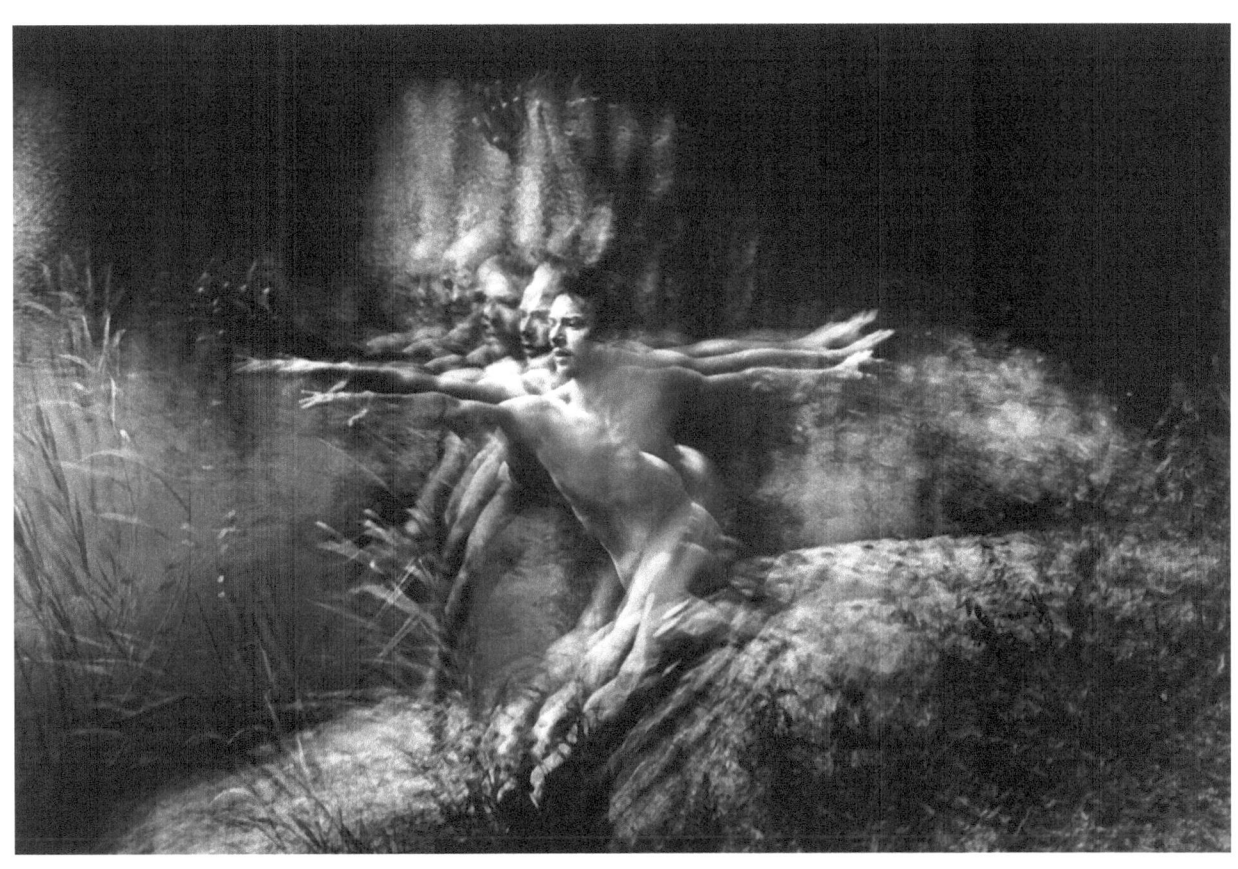

Water Flight Becket, Massachusetts 1998

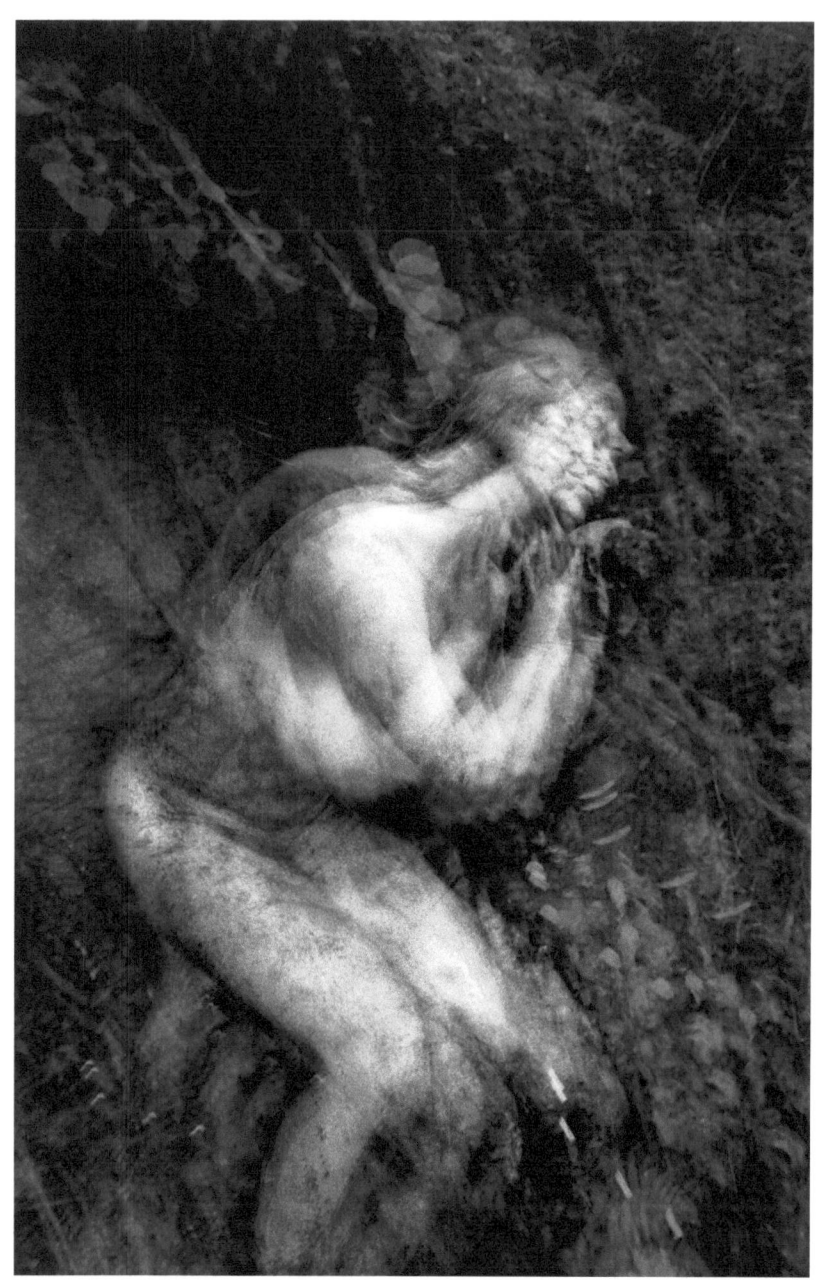

Seeking Solitude Lewiston, Maine 2003

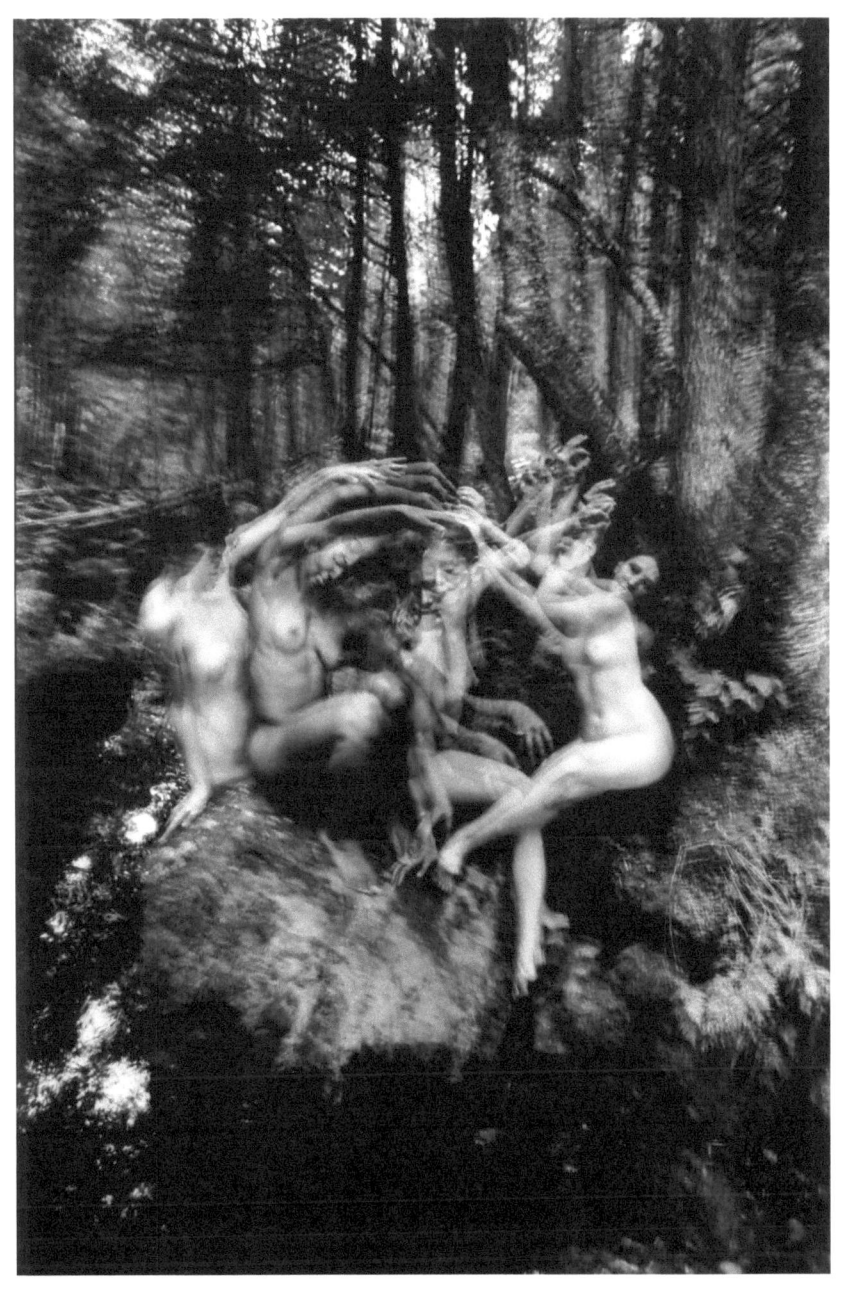

Dancing Dryads Lewiston, Maine 2002

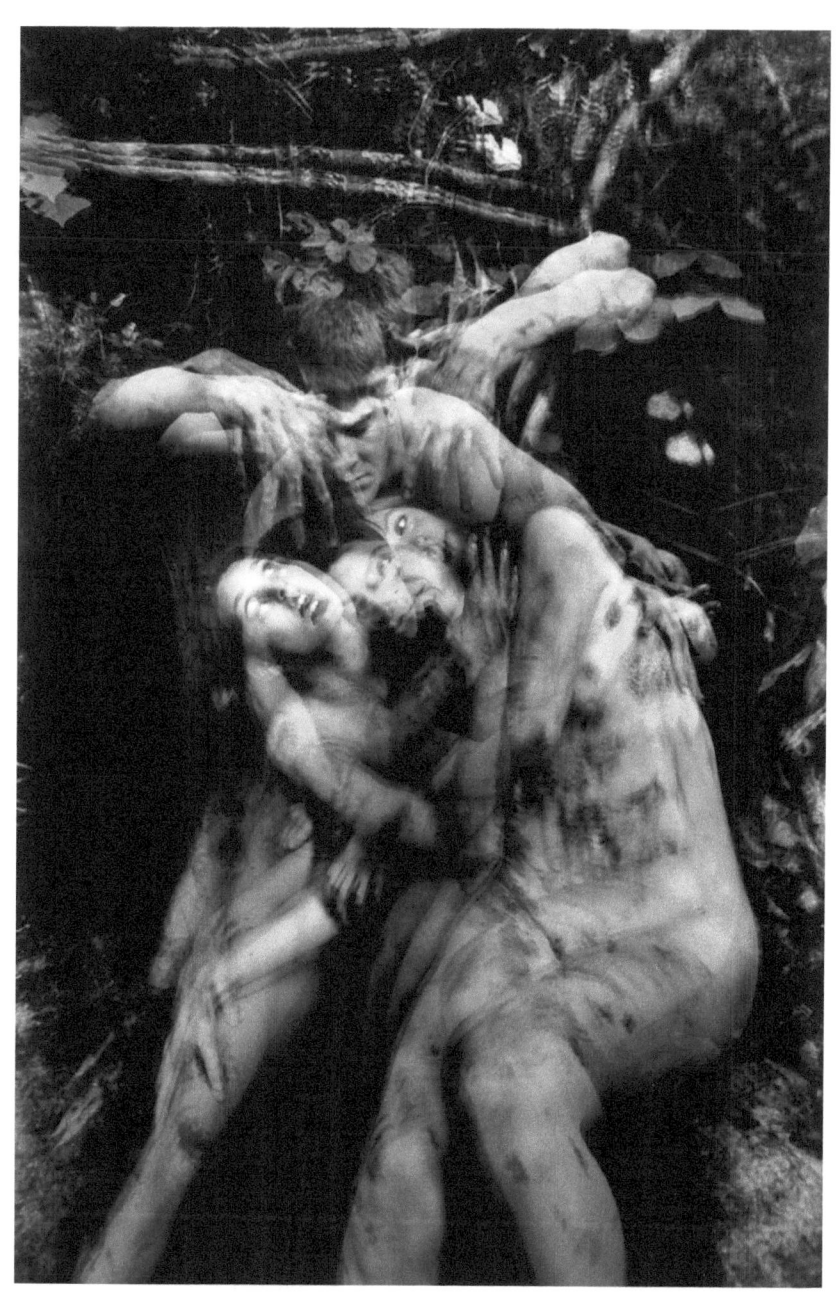

Gates of Hell Lewiston, Maine 2004

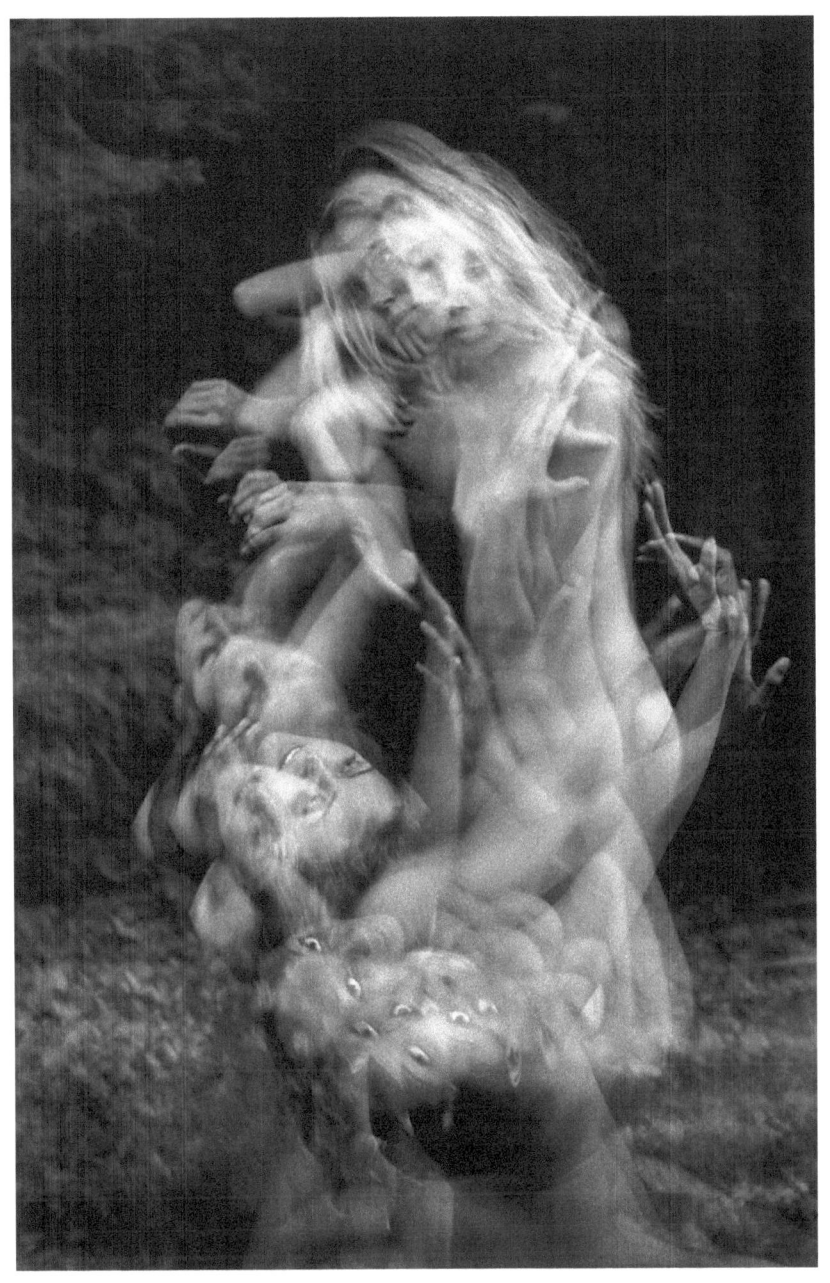

Ovoid Lewiston, Maine 2002

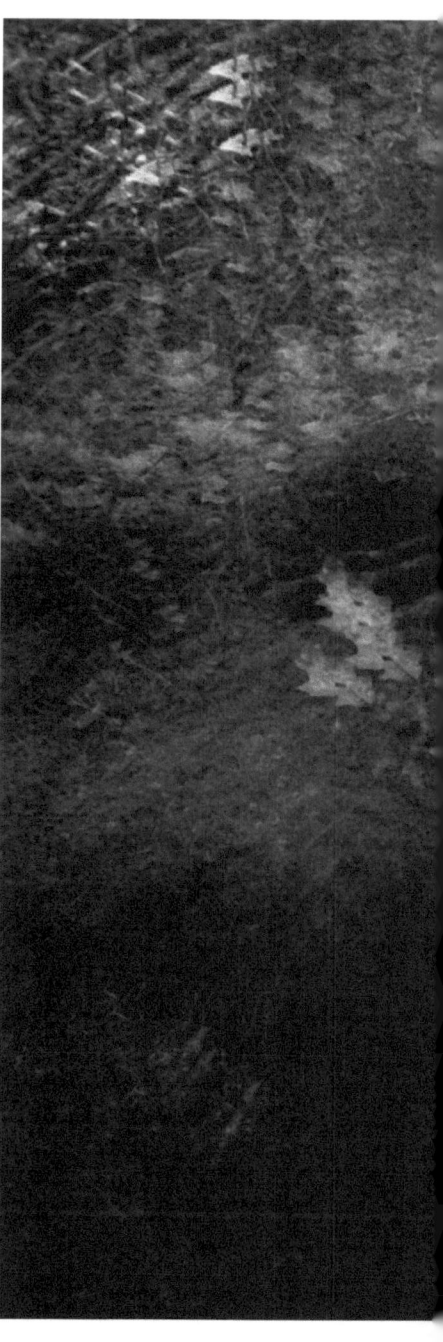

Soft Desire Lewiston, Maine 2002

14

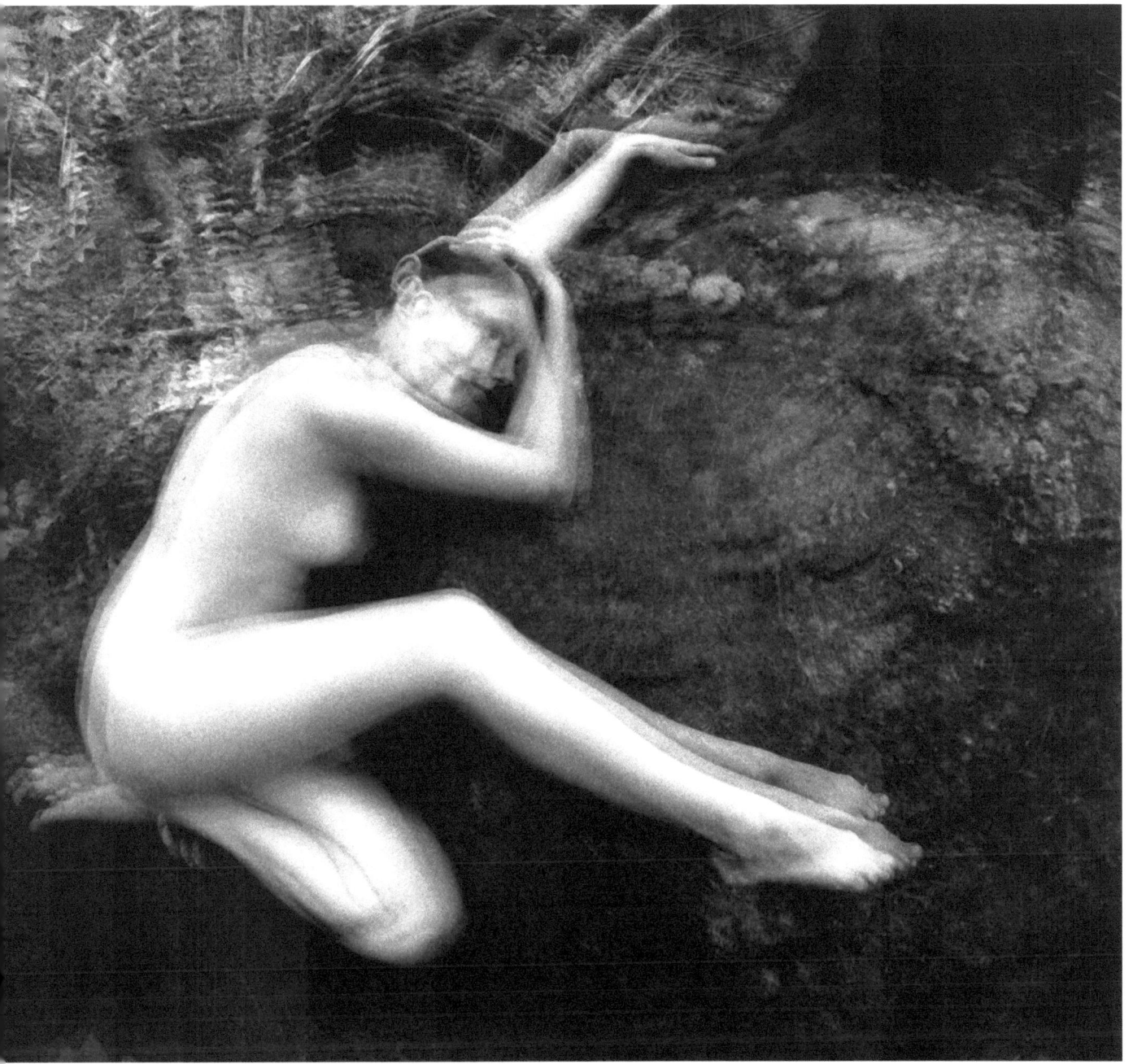

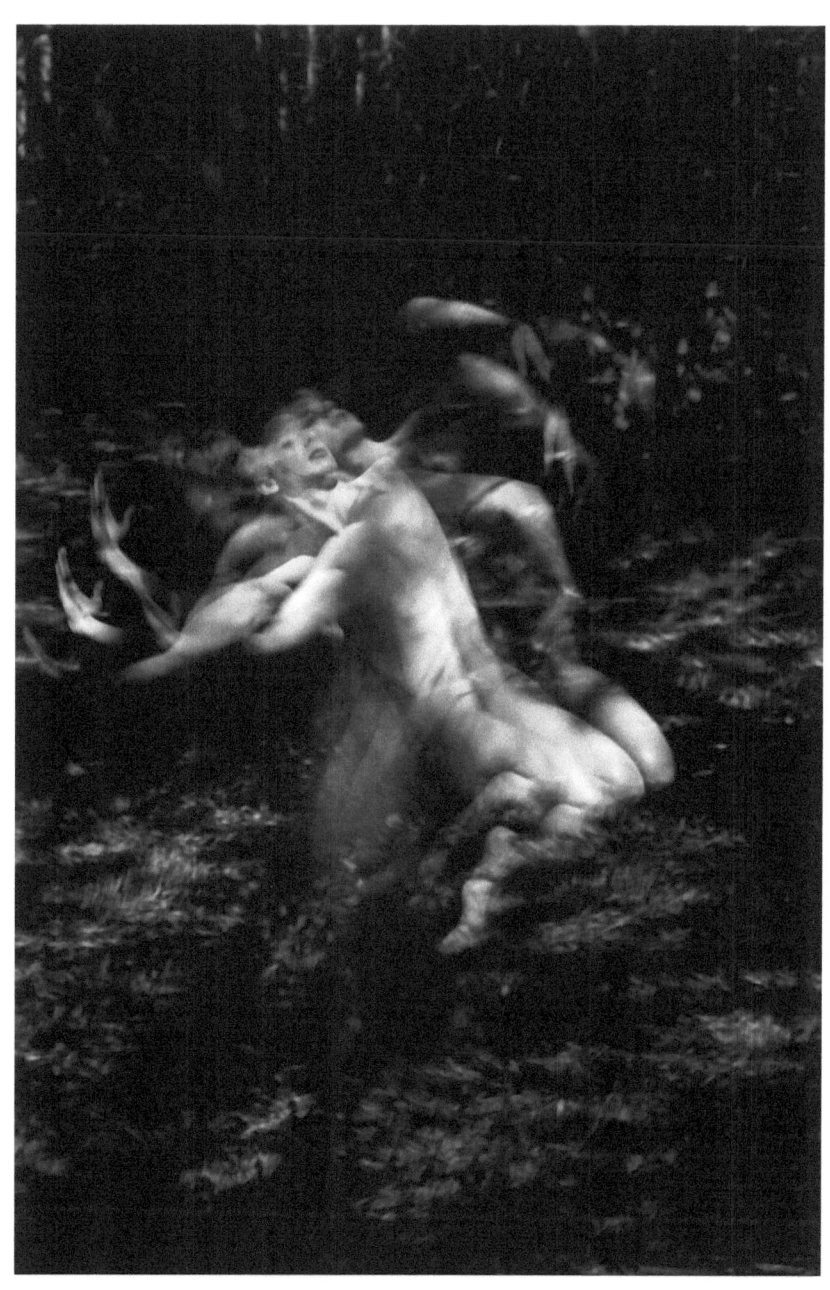

Puck Natick, Massachusetts 1999

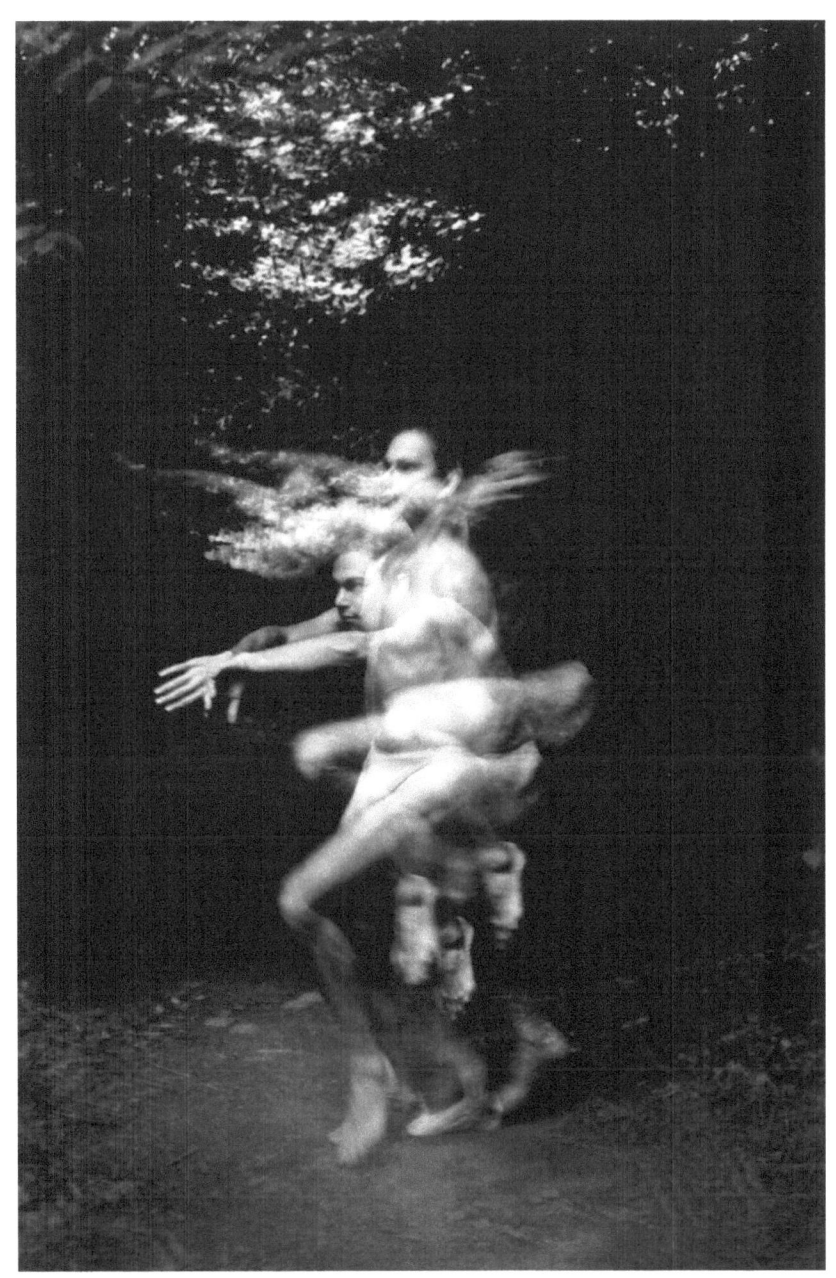

Angel Thrust Saratoga Springs, New York 1999

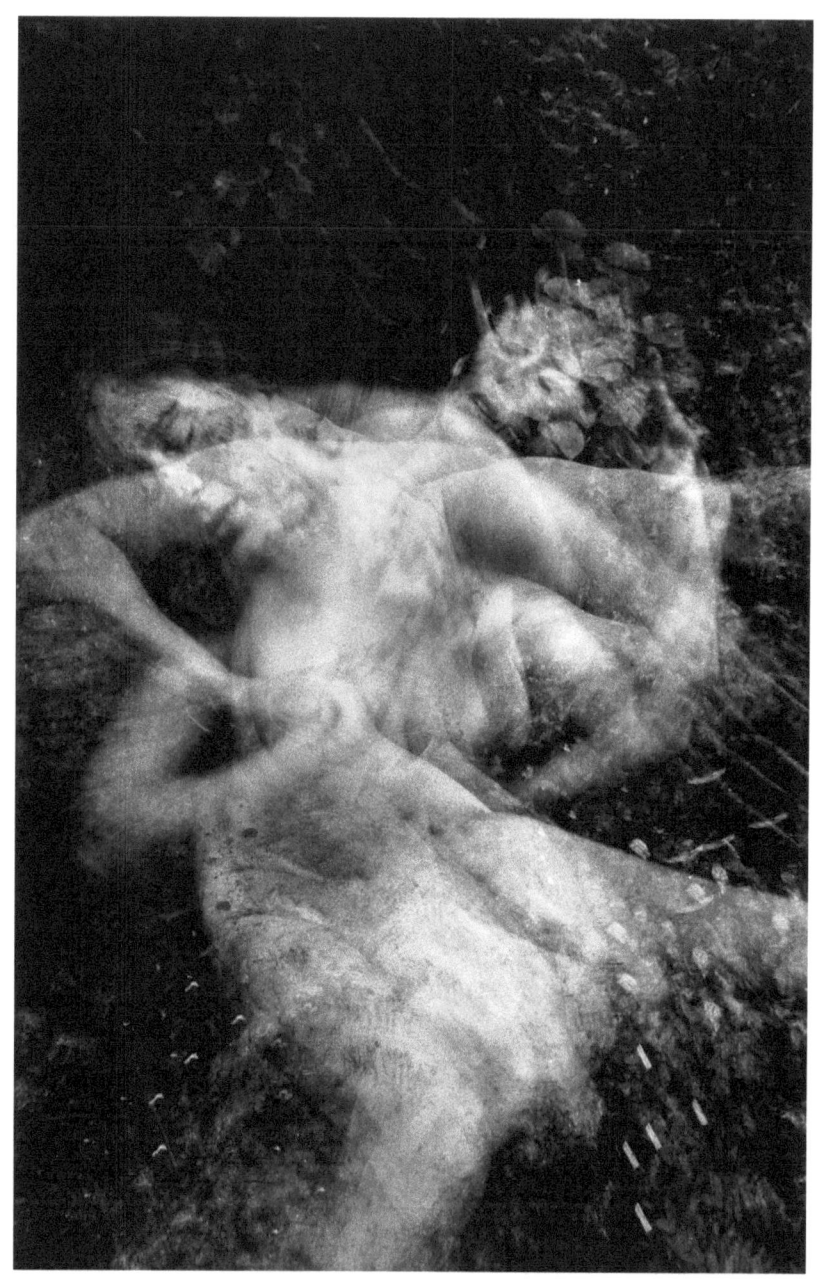

Genie Lewiston, Maine 2003

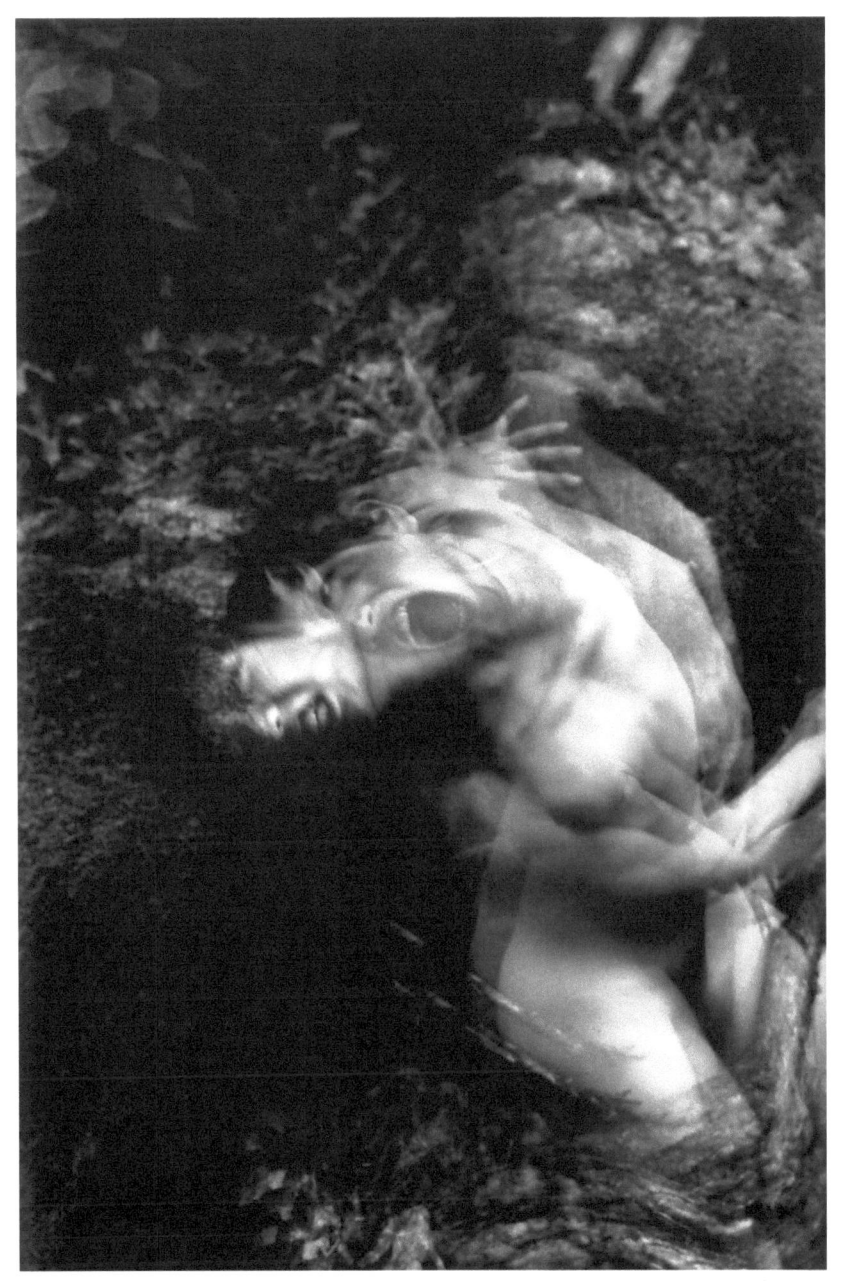

Wail Lewiston, Maine 2004

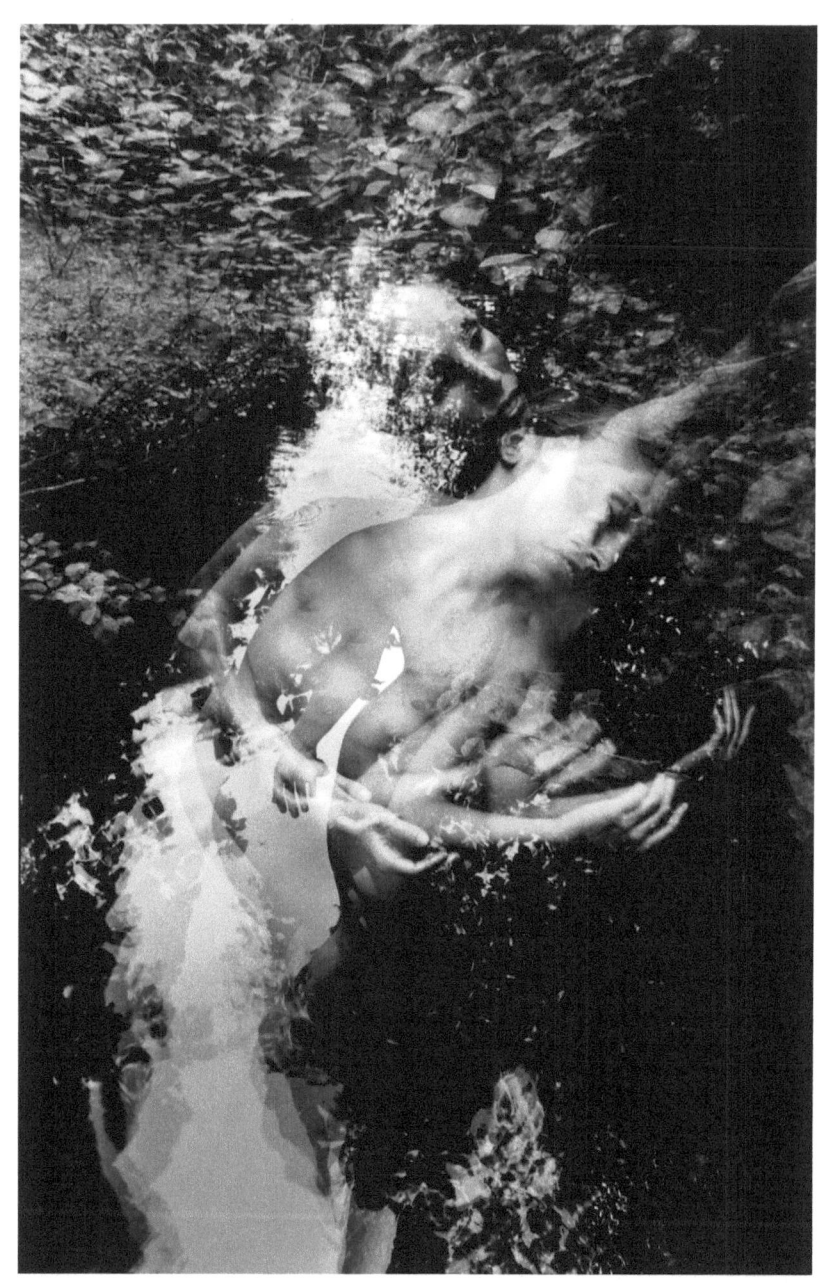

Whispering Hope Lewiston, Maine 2003

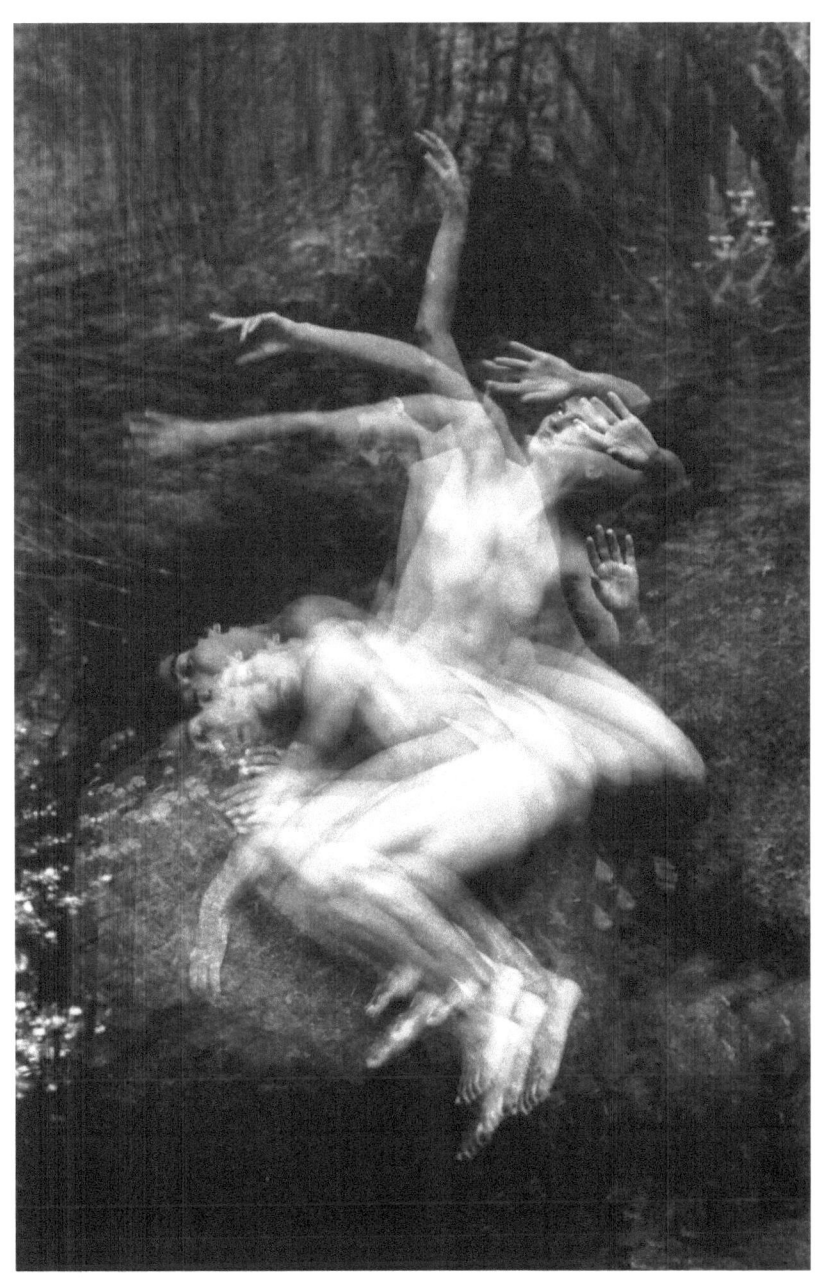

The Protectress Lewiston, Maine 2002

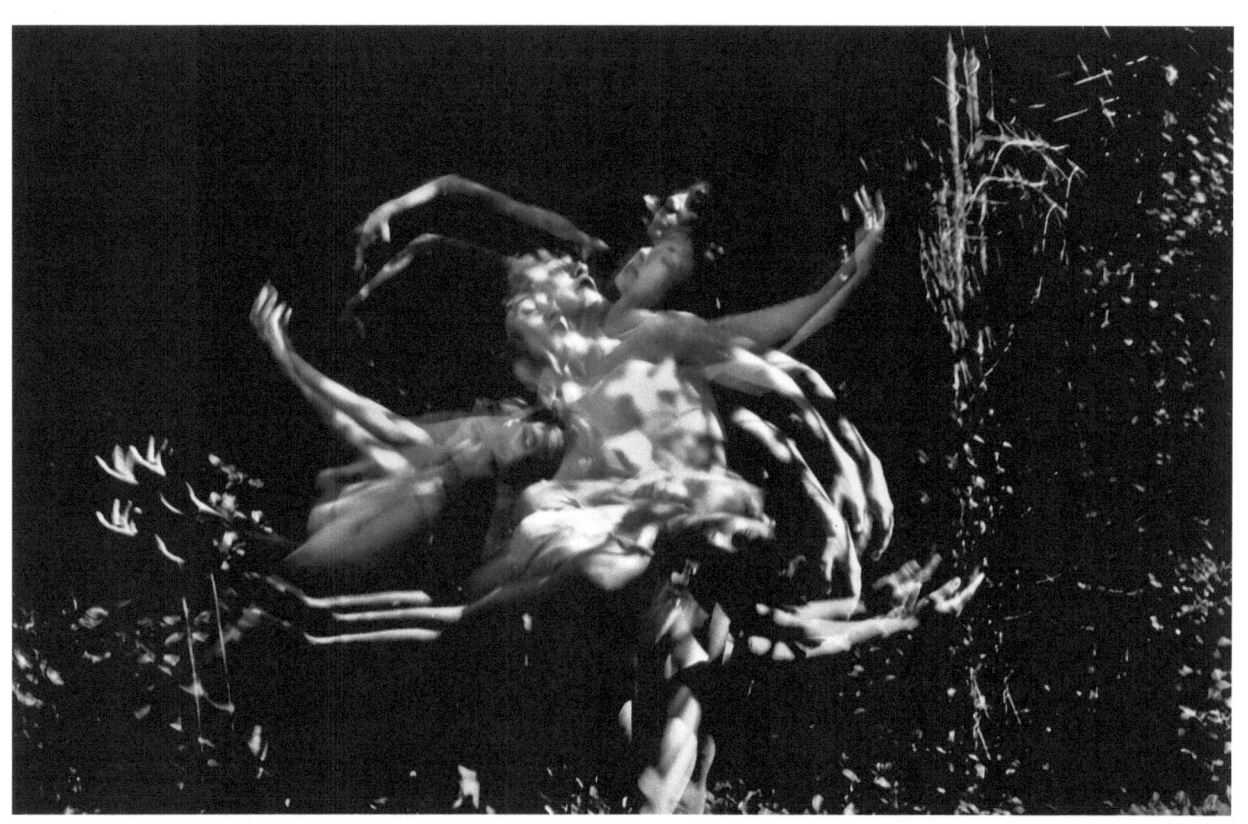

Blossom Saratoga Springs, New York 1999

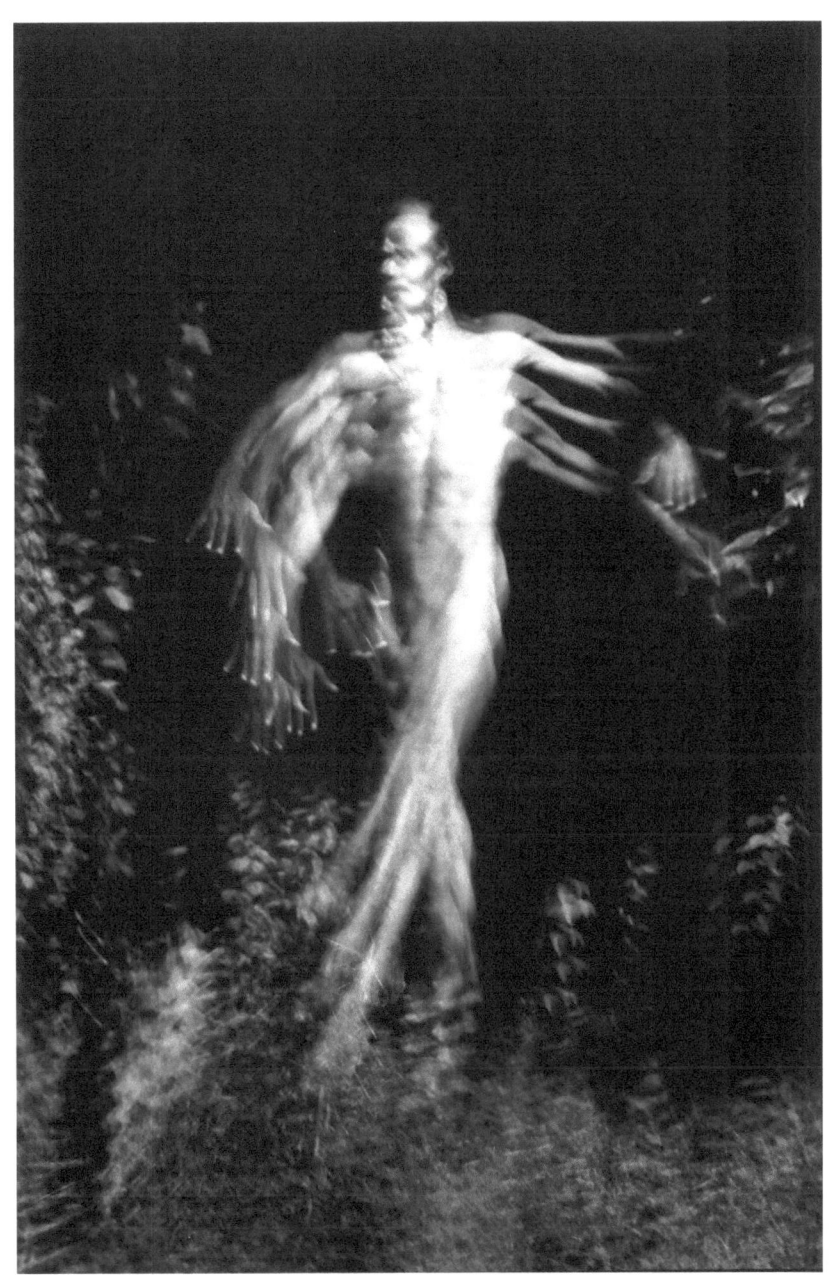

Being Tree Becket, Massachusetts 1998

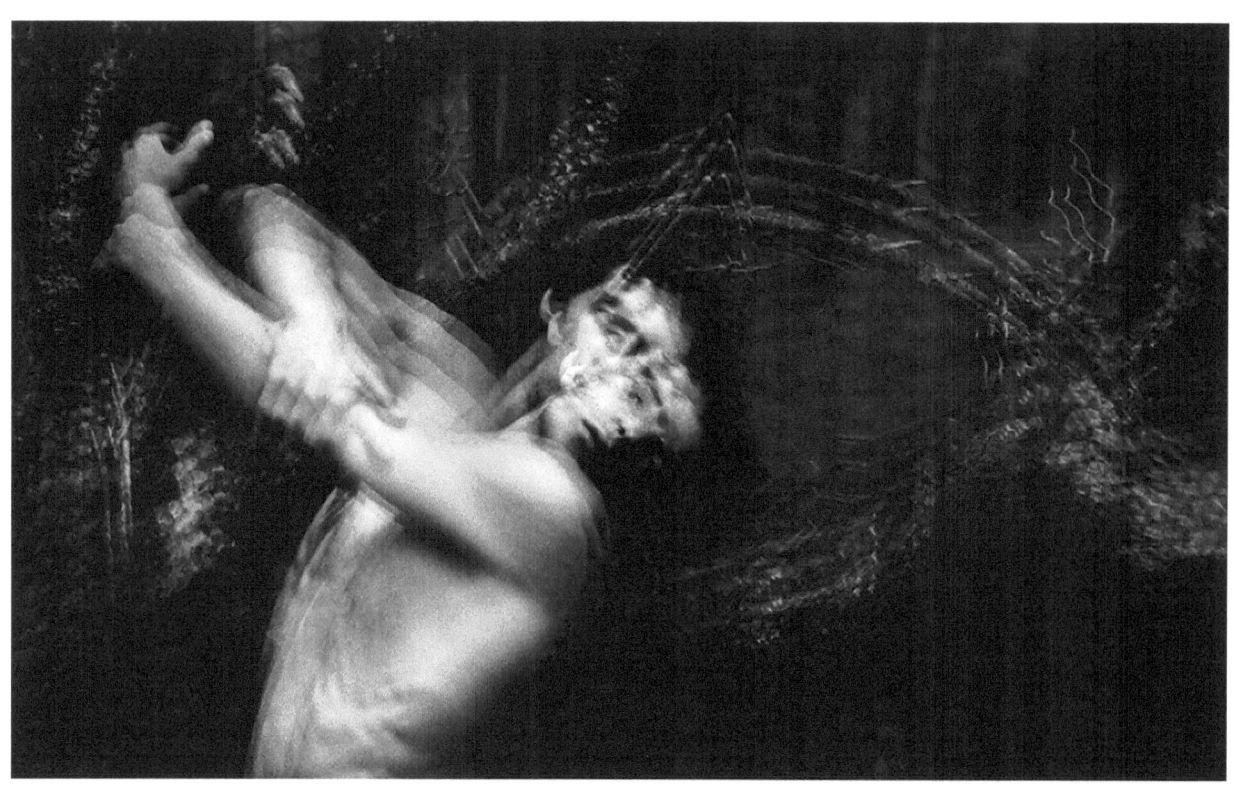

Twist Lewiston, Maine 2003

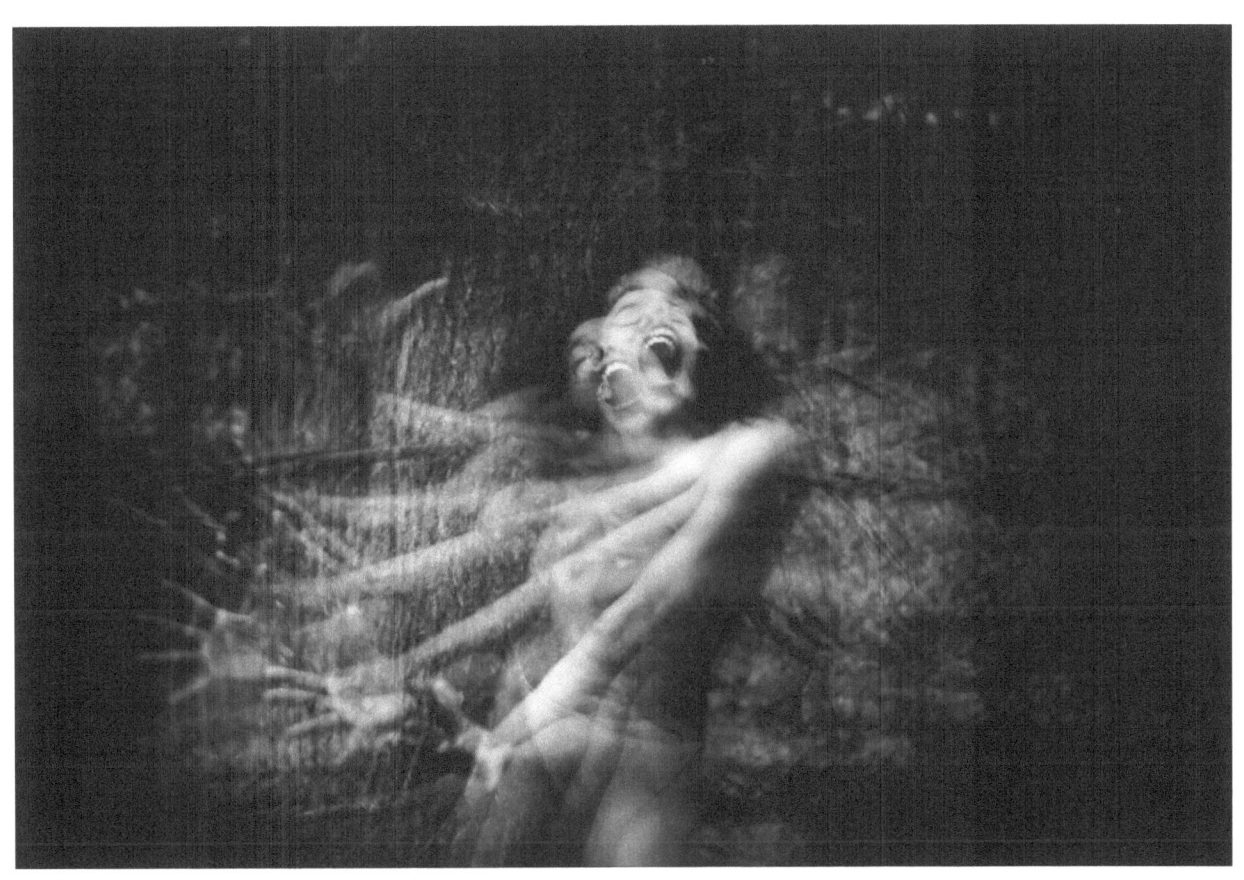

Sing Hallelujah Concord, Massachusetts 2000

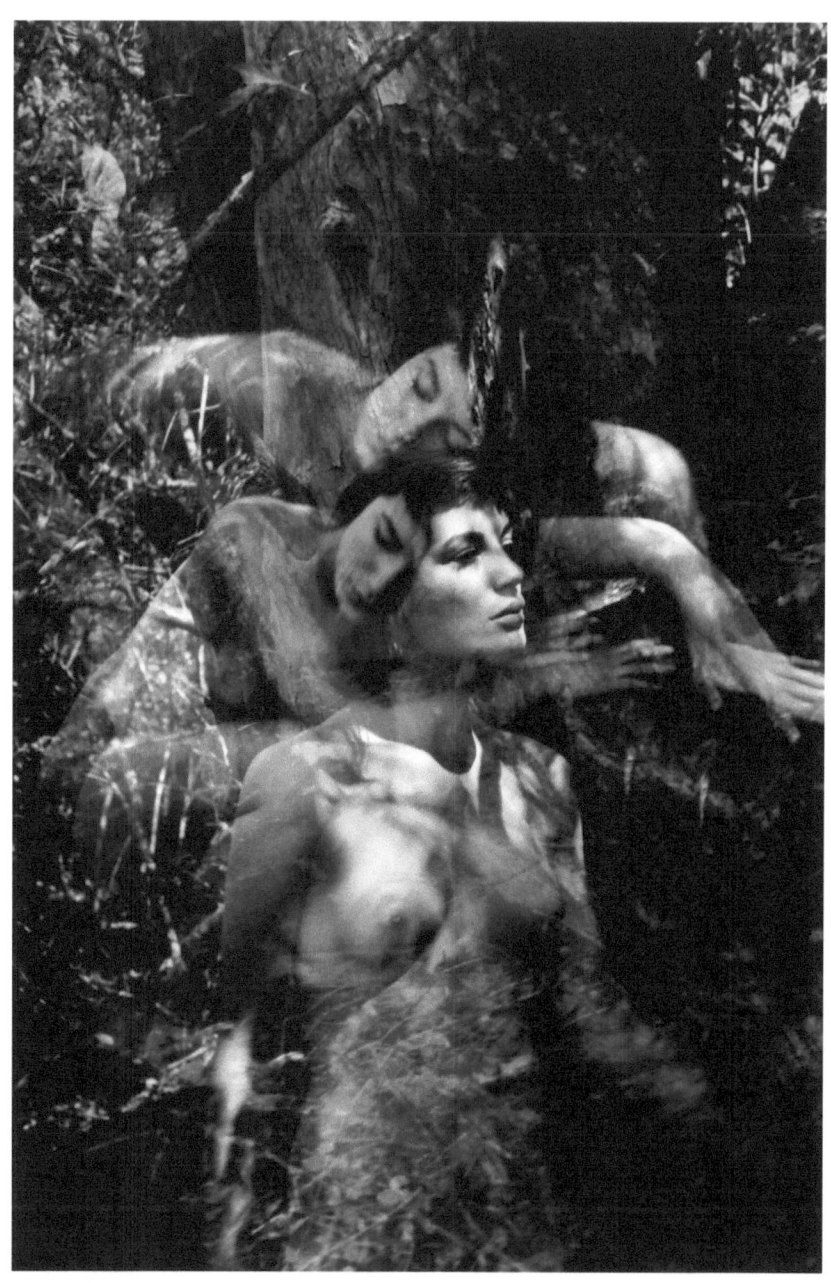

Guarding Innocence South Hadley, Massachusetts 2004

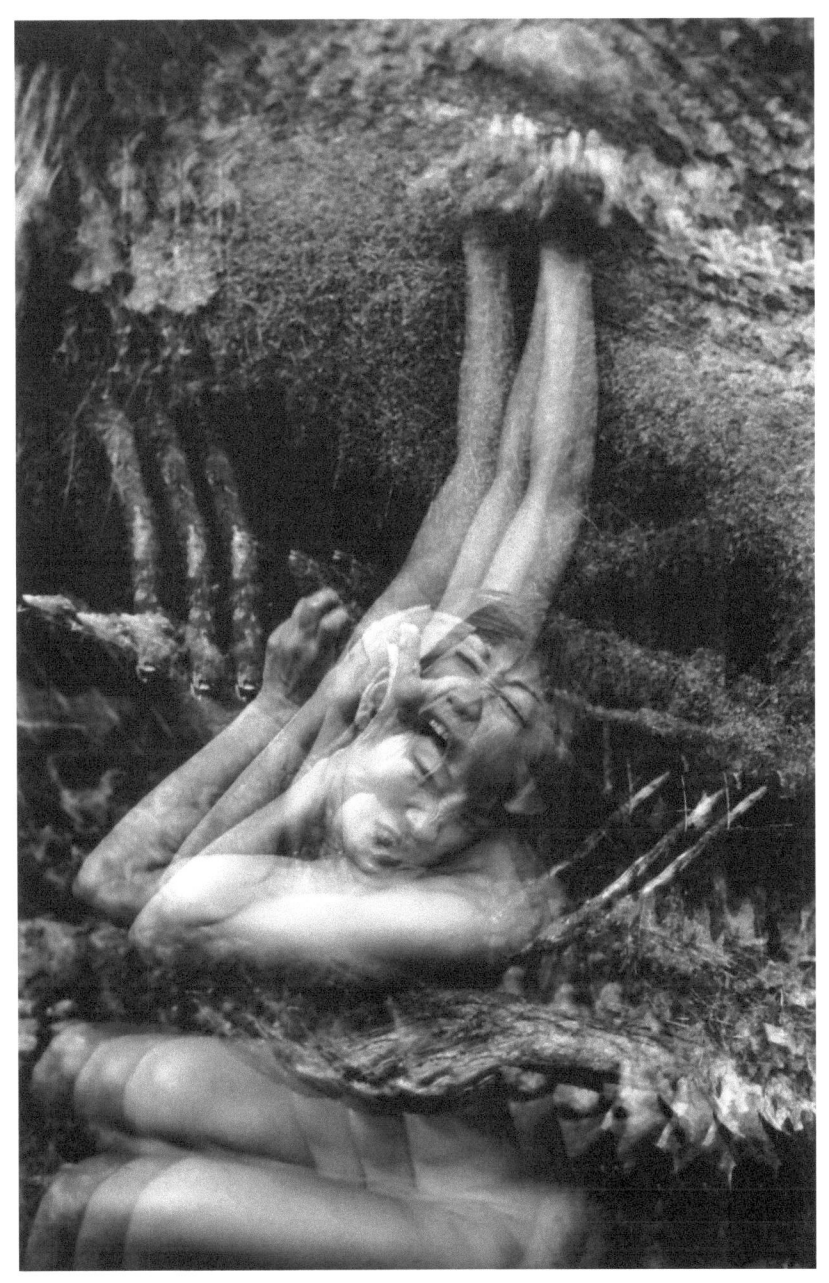

Scream Lewiston, Maine 2004

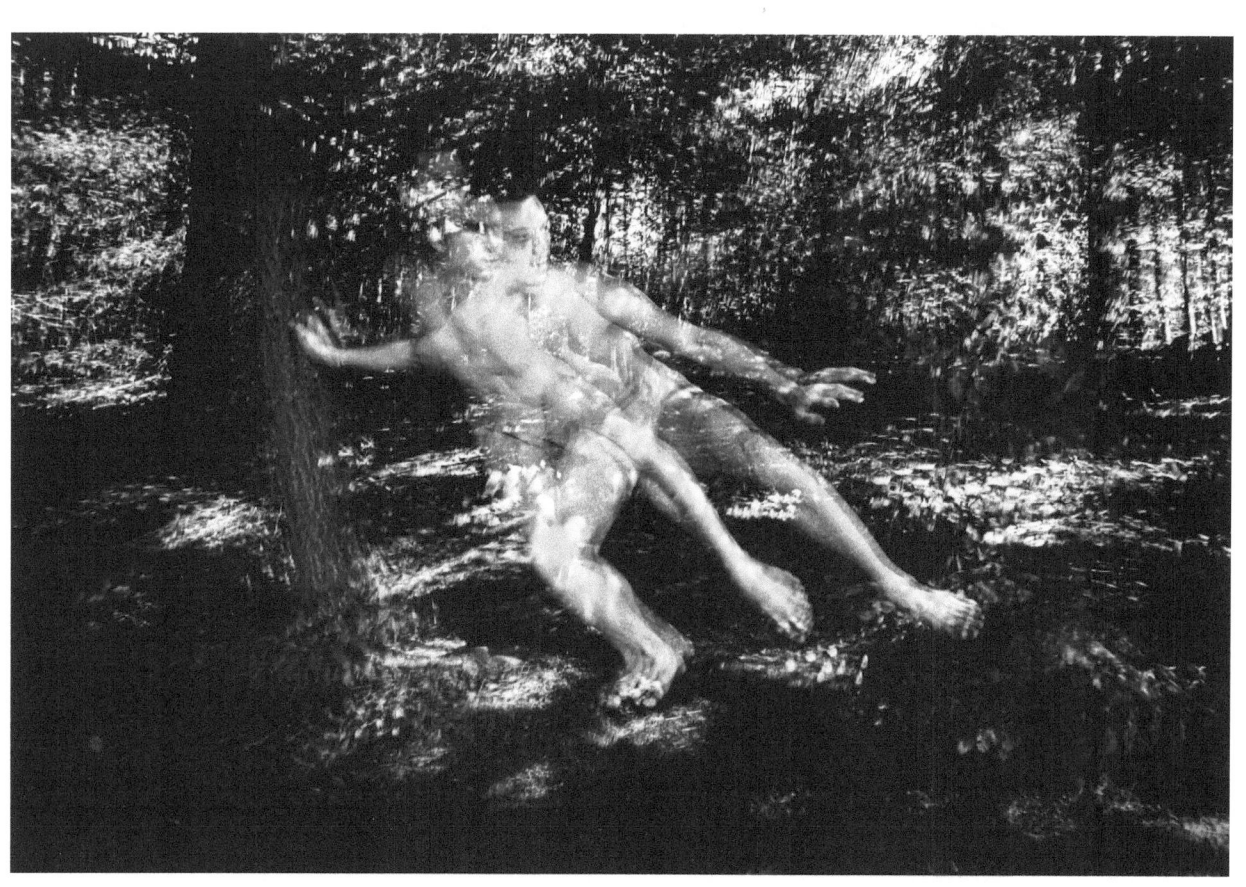

Panther Step Becket, Massachusetts 1998

A Look at the Process and How it Evolved

Watching a 1997 performance of the Limon Dance Company, I had an epiphany: the multi-imagery method I had been developing since 1988 might bring a new dimension to the photography of dance.

My thought was to capture a whole phrase of movement, rather than a single moment. I wanted to put the feel of a performance onto a frame of film, in overlapping layers. In *Under Nature's Canopy*, my prior project, I had photographed the body in motion as an interpretation of the connection between humanity and nature. So I had a feeling for working in nature, and realized that it was the right setting for the organic properties of dance.

I started *The Energy of Dance* in 1998. I photographed members of the Limon Dance Company, initially performing segments of their choreography. When the Limon dancers realized how my multiple exposures could capture the essence of their movement, they began to improvise. As I became aware of this additional dimension that they were offering me, I reacted rather than directed. When I introduced chance, we entered a realm of collaboration that went beyond thought.

As each dancer moved spontaneously, I reacted reflexively, adding images one atop another on a single frame, without plan or purpose. In trusting to intuition with all the technical aspects mastered (I had done much experimenting before starting the project), no control was needed, only intuitive reaction. It's almost frightening to go into this meditative approach, because it's fraught with risk. Yet this is where the magic appears.

The emphasis quickly went into moving with feelings that arose from being in nature. Emotion now created the motion as my subjects trusted intuition and established a feeling of presence. So the dance theme evolved into *Rhythm from Within*, the umbrella for all the segments that have appeared.

This is traveling into the inner world, a spiritual journey that produces a primal kind of physical expression. The results make me even more aware of body language as a universal language, one that we all evoke in our daily lives. And then I wonder, can I ever do this again? And the answer is "no," if I'm thinking of repeating. Because next time something absolutely different but just as amazing is bound to occur.

—Michael Philip Manheim

About Michael Philip Manheim

Born in the United States in 1940, Michael Philip Manheim is widely recognized for his documentary work as well as for his innovative multiple exposure photographs. His work has been exhibited throughout the United States and internationally, in over twenty solo and thirty group exhibitions, including at the Association of International Photography Art Dealers (AIPAD), New York, NY; ART NOW FAIR, Miami Beach, FL; Bates College Museum of Art, Lewiston, ME; Danforth Art Museum at Framing-

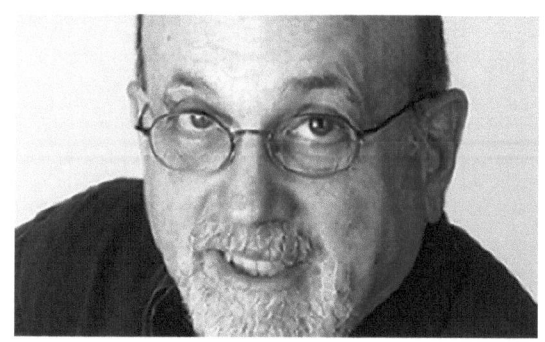

ham State University, Framingham, MA; deCordova Museum and Sculpture Park, Lincoln, MA; Fitchburg Art Museum, Fitchburg, MA; Griffin Museum of Photography, Winchester, MA; Hawai'i Museum of Contemporary Art @ at EHCC, Hilo, HI; International Photography Hall of Fame & and Museum, Oklahoma City, OK; National Museum of Dance, Saratoga Springs, NY; Photographic Resource Center, Boston, MA; and University of Maine Museum of Art, Bangor, ME.

His work has been featured in hundreds of books and magazines such as *Ballet-Tanz* (Germany), *Black and White Magazine* (U.S.); *La Fotografia* (Spain), *Photographers International* (Taiwan), and *Zoom* (U.S. and Italy).

Manheim's photographs are held in private and public collections including the Addison Gallery of American Art, Phillips Academy, Andover, MA; Bates College Museum of Art, Lewiston, ME; Danforth Art Museum at Framingham State University, Framingham, MA; deCordova Museum and Sculpture Park, Lincoln, MA; Fitchburg Art Museum, Fitchburg, MA; International Photography Hall of Fame & Museum, St. Louis, MO; Jacob's Pillow Dance Festival, Becket, MA; Library of Congress, Washington, DC; National Archives and Records Administration, Washington, DC; and University of Maine Museum of Art, Bangor, ME.

Manheim has also participated in residencies at Bates Dance Festival, Bates College, Lewiston, ME; Easton Mountain Retreat, Easton, NY; Pahoa Village Museum, Pahoa, HI; and Phillips Exeter Academy, Exeter, NH.

Michael Philip Manheim lives and works in the Boston area of Massachusetts.

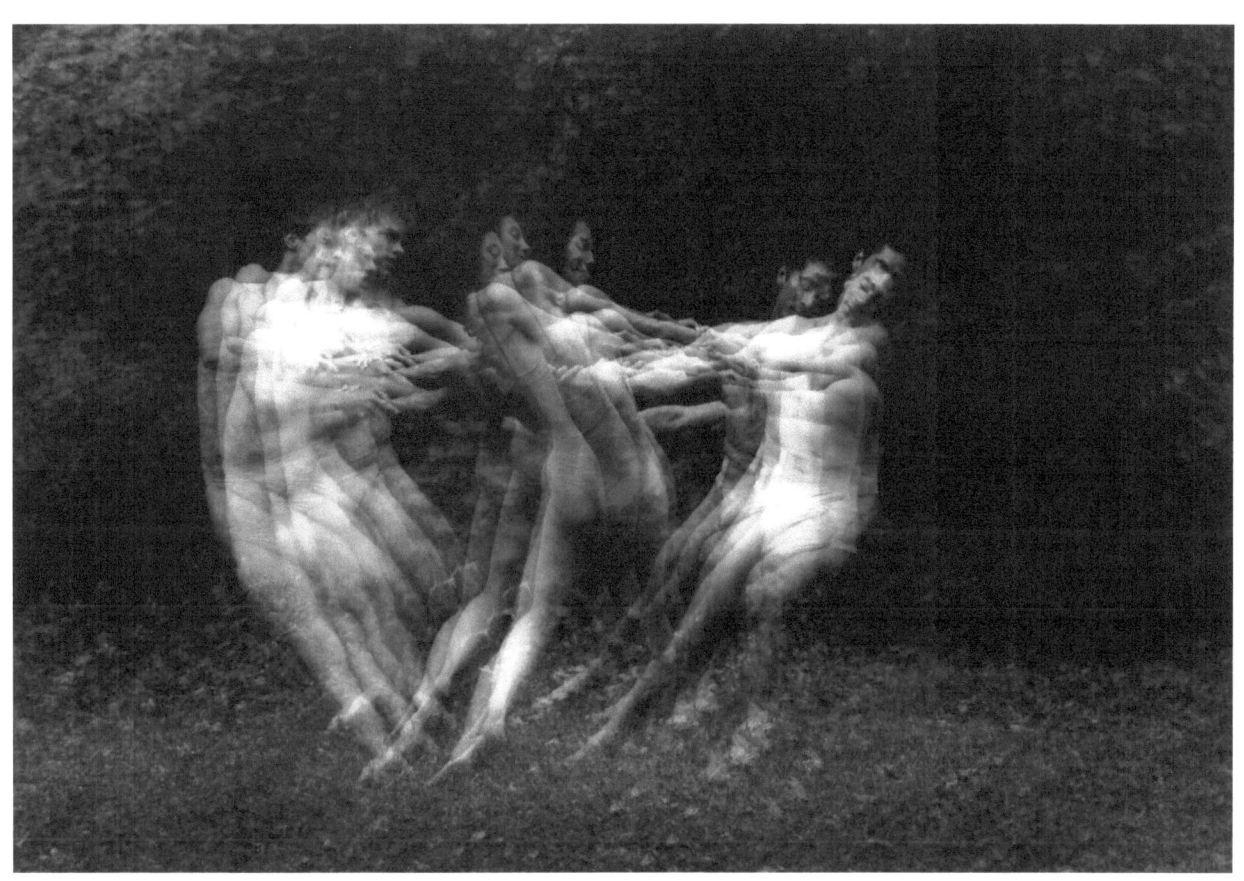

May Dance Becket, Massachusetts 1998